The Future
While
It Happened

BOOKS BY SAMUEL LUBELL

The Future While It Happened
The Hidden Crisis in American Politics
White and Black: Test of a Nation
Revolt of the Moderates
The Revolution in World Trade
The Future of American Politics

SAMUEL LUBELL

The Future
While
It Happened

W · W · NORTON & COMPANY · INC ·

NEW YORK

First Edition

To the many thousands of voters I have interviewed—almost none of whom think they are smart enough to be president— with the hope they will learn to educate our presidents.

Library of Congress Cataloging in Publication Data
Lubell, Samuel.
    The future while it happened.
    1. Presidents—United States—Election—1972.
2. Public opinion—United States. I. Title.
JK526 1972.L8   301.15′43′3209730924   73-5671
ISBN 0 393 05479 9 (Cloth Edition)
ISBN 0 393 09321 2 (Paper Edition)

  2 3 4 5 6 7 8 9 0

Contents

Foreword to the Second Printing

After the Watergate

This book was completed and sent to the printers before the Watergate scandals broke into the open.

The shocking exposures of campaign sabotage, wiretapping espionage, and possible cover-ups demanded correction. Still they provided only a part picture of the crisis of the presidency—much like a body in a snapshot with the head cut off.

What that topless picture lacked is the story told in this book of how the overloaded powers in the White House were used to transform the presidency into a total government in itself, organized for political overkill to get and hold more power.

Even with Richard Nixon out of office this larger crisis of the presidency would persist. Some political reforms being advanced, such as the single six-year presidential term suggested by Nixon, could aggravate the crisis.

The basic fact is that the presidency we thought we knew has changed in disturbing ways. The essence of this transformation lies, I believe, in our having moved into a managed economy with ever-widening executive powers being added while restraints were neglected and crumbled.

To balance and restrain presidential dominance will require reaching beyond political reform to the economic powers of the presidency. As this book emphasizes, how our economy is managed has become the shaping force of the future: abroad, in how our economic lives are integrated into a new global economy being built; at home, in whether a shape-up, squeeze-out psychology continues to determine how taxes, profits, costs of continued inflation, career opportunities—all the rewards and penalties—will be distributed.

Foreword

Phrases like "psychological war" and "total politics" grate on one's eardrums and scrape up images of George Orwell come too soon.

These terms are employed here not in any partisan sense, but to focus sharply on how presidential dominance in managing our society has brought what threatens to become a never-ending psychological contest between the presidency and the American people.

This book examines this struggle between the people and their White House managers, revealing how it has already changed the structure of political and economic power in the country and reshaped much of our future.

Where is this transformation of the presidency taking us? Toward a new unity or more bitter conflict? Toward economic and social stability or deepening troubles?

Actually, this psychological war began with Lyndon Johnson, who, like Nixon, was an agitator-president. The revolutionary innovation added by Nixon was to turn the 1972 presidential contest into our first truly total election, marshaling any and every presidential power to gain support for his actions and policies, dividing and routing the opposition.

Actions taken are emphasized because they contrast so sharply with our habit of thinking that public opinion is shaped primarily through propaganda efforts—speeches and debates, TV theatricals, and varied tricks of image-making.

Newsmen were frustrated with justification when Nixon refused any verbal interchange of views with George McGovern or to answer questions from the press. In a managed society the critical interplay is not verbal debate but actions taken and resistance provoked. Ineffective resistance becomes tantamount to ratification of the action by the voters.

Voter shifts to Nixon heavy enough to re-elect him followed the mining of Haiphong and the bombings of North Vietnam—months before McGovern was nominated. What is done to win the election can be more important than the voting on election day. Total politics could also mean no real end to any election. The voting marks only a brief pause before the battling resumes, which is what has happened in Nixon's second term.

Nixon's handling of the 1974 budget reductions and revenue sharing provides another illustration of the action technique. The cuts in social and urban programs were not debated but were ordered into effect, sometimes with the hatchetlike dispatch of Carrie Nation, as with the poverty programs.

Troubled mayors, governors, and others who were hurt had to fight back, which tested the strength of their resistance. In many communities, rival claimants—libraries against fire departments, day-care centers against police cars—fought over revenue-sharing funds. Which programs would draw sufficient support to force a Nixon backdown? Which would stir few defenders and lose out completely?

How does one go about reporting a total election? My findings reflect how the voters themselves, interviewed in twenty-one states, reacted to the many White House manipulations.

When I began my interviewing, I did not have a full grasp of what a total election meant. Still, twenty years of election reporting had given me a considerable understanding of the psychological processes by which voters identify with and reject candidates and issues.

Then, each election is always a new learning experience for me. My methodology of intensive interviewing in carefully selected precincts—described fully in the Appendix—is organized to catch changes in voter feeling from one election to the next and to work out their meaning.

A total election, it soon turned out, shared some qualities of total war, in that everything had importance—but in varied ways.

I came to look upon each voter as three-dimensional— part of the terrain of political manipulation; a target for psychological attack; and a combatant on one side, as the nation divided, with Americans voting against other Americans.

Racial conflict was the sharpest cleavage by far—with "welfare" serving as 1972's code word for anti-Negro—spurring more voter shifts to Nixon than any other single issue.

Hair was another target of considerable voter wrath and job discrimination. One long-haired youth from St. Petersburg, Florida, recalled, "When I left school, the only job I could get was shoveling chicken manure at $1.30 an hour."

Other complaints ran: "The longer your hair, the rougher it is to get the better jobs," or "They won't hire you unless they can hide you."

The suburbs became much more than crab-grass preserves where the heaviest concentrations of white voters lived. They were also the decisive battlefield over school busing, where an interviewer could determine whether it was just busing that was opposed—or were people using the issue to end all integration?

For the future, the suburbs remain a site of treacherous political temptation. The black-white separation from the "inner city" becomes a political force in itself, luring many suburbanites into thinking, "keep the blacks inside the cities," and "forget the whole racial problem."

It is a treacherous temptation because the shift of jobs to the suburbs threatens to aggravate racial conflict.

It was the eighteen-year-olds who provided one key to the whole "total election" puzzle. Nearly all these youths shared the identical problem of fitting themselves into the economy, either on immediate jobs or in future careers. How they fitted in—or didn't—showed up as perhaps the strongest single factor shaping their political feelings.

By early September, I wrote that the "new Nixon majority" could best be described as "the shape-up coalition," warm and rewarding if one shaped up, cold and McGovernish if one did not, or if one couldn't find a secure job in the economy.

For adults as well, our interview findings indicated that Nixon's control of the economy had become the prime force structuring—and dividing—the voting.

After the election the reductions in the 1974 budget dug these divisions deeper. Defense increases and cuts in social programs were lined up in open confrontation as if they were mortal enemies.

What meaning was to be put on the election results as to where the President is moving the country?

On this I was constantly impressed by the gap between Nixon's rhetoric and how the voters interpreted what he said. His anti-tax and anti-government talk bristled with toughness about the "work ethic," the need for discipline, the need to become more competitive. To the voters all this somehow got translated into demands for "more" in the way of personal gain on their part. Nor did this drive of "every man for himself" strengthen our ability to export more abroad.

A chapter on the welfare issue reveals how competitive individualism operates to push out of sight what is weakest and most vulnerable; also, much anti-welfare feeling reflected a desire to get the medical benefits from the government that the welfare recipients were getting for nothing.

Other chapters show how the ideology of economic individualism, while increasing incentive, is almost a new form of government which enables voters to cut away from unwanted or unmanageable burdens and to push off onto others the costs of continued inflation.

A chapter on the military-industrial job complex discusses how an unbalanced domestic economy threatens to undercut any peace and defense policy that is undertaken.

One major conclusion was the decisive importance of the power to commit the country's future. Once the fishhook of commitment becomes lodged in a nation's throat, voter opinion will thrash about furiously, like a powerful but helpless sailfish.

This, of course, was the story of the Vietnam war. By sending B-52 bombers over North Vietnam in 1965, Lyndon Johnson committed us to a vast escalation of a war that thrashed on for seven years, even though most Americans felt, "It was a mistake to ever get in." Under both Johnson and Nixon the drive for presidential power has been a drive to commit the future.

On George McGovern's role, too much of the Democratic debacle has been heaped on him. He was hurt far more by his "welfare plan" than by the Eagleton affair. Still, for a man who thought he spoke for the people, his campaigning revealed little sensitivity to how the public felt about the major conflicts at issue.

In contrast, Nixon's campaigning always touched the emotions that agitated and divided the nation. Repeatedly, voters would begin an interview by voicing doubts or misgivings about Nixon, but usually his record on at least some one major conflict brought him their support.

Ours being a psychological age, many efforts will be made to explain the Nixon performance in terms of personality and even psychiatry.

Still, the fact that his administration brought a total election really reflects three forces:

The turbulent divisions over race and war that developed in the 1960s.

Vast new powers, particularly in managing the economy, that were added to the presidency in this same period.

The technological abundance and the wealth—real and printed—that was produced in the last decade. For 1971, Federal Reserve estimates put the net worth of U.S. households at $3.5 trillion, double what it was in 1960.

The mixing bowl of power into which Nixon agitated these elements will have to be changed, I believe, to survive politically. Above all, what the Nixon majority needs today is effective resistance. Still, much of the future has already happened to us.

March 1973

Acknowledgments

THE WRITING OF THIS BOOK would not have been possible without the devoted and extremely effective assistance of Juyne Kaupp, my right-arm aide. Her sensitive interviewing brightens many of the pages; no part of this book is without her improving touch.

I am deeply indebted to Evan Thomas for his patient editing of the manuscript, as well as to his girl Friday and every other day in the week, Rose Franco.

On the attitudes of young voters, Gail and David Weber were particularly helpful with three classroom surveys at the Palisades High School in Bucks County, Pennsylvania, as was William Lobb, their interested principal. William A. Ivy organized a similar survey at the Forrest City High School in Arkansas, as did Rosalind Eisner at Birmingham High School near Los Angeles.

Professor William R. Nelson of Memphis State University was always readier than a fireman to arrange for special surveys of key precincts in Memphis from 1970 through 1972.

In Washington, Joseph A. Pechman and Charles Schultz have been invaluable in discussing fiscal problems; also, I have turned repeatedly to Calvin Beale of the Department of Agriculture, Henry D. Sheldon at the Census Bureau, and Joseph Loftus, Hyman Kaitz, and Denis F. Johnston at the Labor Department. Alan Severn of the Federal Reserve and Edward Bernstein were particularly helpful on world economic problems.

Nancy Moore and John Goolrick, both with the *Free Lance–Star*, were especially helpful with information about Fredericksburg, Virginia. Peter Kihss and Glenn Gerstell did yeoman work with New York City's new assembly districts. William Gilbert of the York *Dispatch* helped in his city.

For interviewing help during the 1972 campaign, I'm grateful to William H. Kusewich and Steven Graves; for a *Look* magazine survey of eighteen-year-olds, Karl Inderfurth and Daniel DiBenedetto; for a 1970 survey in New York, James Wannless, Glenda Rosenthal, Walter Lubell, and Aileen Jacobson.

Assisting me in gathering voting returns were Douglas LaFollette in Kenosha, Wisconsin, Corinne Kyle in Philadelphia, and Jack Welsh, registration supervisor in Philadelphia.

On the Washington *Star-News*, where I supervised a special election survey, it was good to work with Newbold Noyes, Charles Seib, David Kraslow, Harvey Kabaker, and Ronald Paci.

A Ford Foundation grant was of valuable assistance in preparing the summary of my methodology in the Appendix. This grant was exhausted in 1971. No part of it was used in my 1972 election coverage.

My 1972 reports were syndicated by the New York Times

Special Features service; John Osenenko was always ready with enthusiastic suggestions.

Among the 115 editors who took my 1972 election series, I feel special warmth for those who have run my election surveys since they began in 1952—my appreciation to Lee Hills and other Knight Newspaper editors, Derick Daniel of the Detroit *Free Press*, George Beebe of the Miami *Herald*, C. A. McKnight of the Charlotte *Observer*, and Perry Morgan of the Akron *Beacon-Journal;* also, to John Quinn and John Omicinski for the fine working arrangement with the Gannett newspaper chain; to Daryle Feldmeir of the Chicago *Daily News;* to John Leard of the Richmond *Times-Dispatch*.

No complete listing is even possible of the many editors who furnished voting returns from their areas. I owe special thanks to Robert J. Leeny of the New Haven *Register*, David Starr of the *Long Island Press*, George Carmack of the Albuquerque *Tribune*, Charles Whiteford and Peter Sensenbaugh of the Baltimore *Sun*, Mason Walsh of the Phoenix *Gazette*, Mike Maidenburg of the Detroit *Free Press*, Joe Seacrest of the Lincoln *Journal*, Arthur Deck of the Salt Lake *Tribune*, Brady Black of the Cincinnati *Enquirer*, Charles Egger of the Columbus *Journal*, John Troan of the Pittsburgh *Press*, Robert J. Haiman of the St. Petersburg *Times*, William Pulsifer of the Rochester *Times Union*, J. A. Clendinen of the Tampa *Tribune*, Claude Sitton of the Raleigh *News & Observer*, Joseph Dunn of the Norfolk *Virginian-Pilot*, Kenneth MacDonald of the Des Moines *Register*.

Elizabeth Milbrandt was helpful in many emergencies.

Finally, to my wife, Helen Sopot Lubell, there is no adequate way to express my appreciation for her patience and endurance in seeing through still another book.

————◄••••►————

As THIS BOOK was being locked up, Walker Stone, former editor-in-chief of Scripps-Howard Newspapers, died. Little known to the public, he was a truly great editor. It was he who, in 1952, backed me in what was then an untried form of election reporting—solely by talking to the voters themselves.

As an editor he handled me perfectly from a reporter's point of view. First of all, he read my copy. Every now and then he would telephone me about my reports. Once he woke me up in Chicago to say, "Sam, you're writing as if Eisenhower is going to win by a landslide but we are getting reports that Kentucky is staying Democratic. It's never happened before that a President won by a landslide and still lost the border states."

I replied, "I don't know what's happening in Kentucky but I have been interviewing in Chicago and Eisenhower is cutting in heavily on the Democratic vote."

I will never forget what Walker told me when it came time to wind up that series. He said I didn't have to make any prediction on the winner. It was nice to have the pressure taken off in that way, and it was tempting to keep from going out on a limb. But after a moment's thought, I told Walker, "Here I have been going around the country for three and a half months. If I don't have any idea who is going to win, my readers have a right to ask, what have I been doing?"

And so—at that time most forecasts were for a close race —I wrote that Eisenhower would win by a landslide. That is how I got to be an election prophet.

Through all the elections that followed, until Walker's retirement in 1969, we never had a written agreement—and we never had a misunderstanding.

Chapter I

A Tale of Modern Feudalism

1. The Purity Crusade

AFTER THE Democratic presidential convention in Miami, I was puzzled how one might convey to readers an understanding of the unusual contest that lay ahead between George McGovern and Richard Nixon.

About that time I chanced upon an illustrated monograph describing huge wall-sized murals that an artist had painted of a tremendous struggle for power that had once taken place in a mythical land which historians often referred to as "The Brave New Feudal World."

The artist had entitled his murals *Plains of Anger and Castles of Power.*

On the Plains the central scene was one of tumultuous commotion amidst many tents as the Insurgent Evangelist and his long-haired aides moved among the outpourings of blacks, Chicanos, and other pagan minorities of discontent, exhorting them with visions of a victorious assault upon the Castles, to spread out into the furthest reaches, enrolling friends, parents, and all whose voices were not usually heard.

Inside the main Castle—some feudalists called it the Big White House—the scene centered on the office of the medieval Board Chairman, working at a desk swept clean except for yellow monastery-sized pads, on which he noted meticulously the many actions to be taken to mobilize every bit of available political power that could be reached.

Noted down, of course, were the orders customarily issued before every election to all allied Castles; to wit, make work for registered voters (giving preference to those with large families) by filling all moats that were empty and emptying all moats that might be full, repairing drawbridges, cleaning turrets and battlements, tearing up some roadways and patching others.

But for this historic struggle for power the Board Chairman had also contrived many new and ingenious arrangements with hitherto hostile Baronies of Labor and Castles to the South that still flew the flag of the opposition forces.

If the Evangelist were to win, goodly numbers of Castle supporters had to be persuaded to join him, no matter how prodigious his youthful levies might prove to be.

To accomplish this, his main "strategy" seemed to lie in trying to shame the Board Chairman, a notoriously secretive fellow, into open encounter with "I dare you" taunts of "Come out and joust the issues with me," or "Send out your biggest giants," or "Why do you send before the people nothing more than surrogate vassals?"

Possibly the Evangelist hoped to re-enact a biblical tale which had fascinated him in childhood, that of David and

Goliath, thus discrediting with one slingshot stone the Board Chairman along with the sundry pollster-magicians who were thicker than usual in the land.

For the Board Chairman, the obvious strategy would be to frighten the voters into hugging more tightly the promised security of the Castle walls by picturing the Evangelist as a "scare" figure who threatened new taxes on all properties and capital gains, and would render idle all manner of ordnance mechanics, defense technicians, and many others.

In short, the Board Chairman set out to make the Evangelist seem intent upon bringing down the whole system of walls, as had once happened in the United States of Jericho.

The more furious and despairing the Insurgent Evangelist was made to appear, the Board Chairman reasoned, the more entrenched the Castles of Power would become, even to being able to dominate the Plains of Anger to a vaster degree than ever before.

This, verily, is what came to pass.

As oft happens with great defeats or victories, curious legends grew up as to how the Evangelist was subjugated. Most widely circulated of these tales was one that attributed his misfortune to an awkward handling of a certain matter concerning Sir Thomas of Eagleton, whose knighthood was deflowered because he had been psychoanalyzed.

Now, the Evangelist had indeed been afflicted with knighthood troubles—but it was not from any pointy-head tilter at windmills. The Evangelist's nemesis was the Knight on the Yellow School Bus, who had come charging into the Plains from the South, thrusting his anti-tax and anti-color lances to the right and left with gusto and zeal.

And as the Knight on the Yellow School Bus rampaged through the Plains of Anger, it was astonishing to behold how the discontented divided against one another along such feudal variables as complexion, taxable income bracket, color of collar worn at work, or number of books read.

Much aggrieved and wroth, the Evangelist is said to have turned upon his own pollster-magician, one Caddell Merlin III, a youthful graduate of the Harvard School of Sorcery Administration, and demanded, "Didn't you swear by your sorcery ring that everyone in this domain was under a deep spell of anti-Castle alienation? It seemeth that they all are bewitched into alienation against me."

The simple truth was that when the Evangelist entered the primary tournaments, he was concerned only with defeating the older knights. It would seem that he, the Evangelist, had not really expected to be anointed to lead the Crusade of Purity against the Castle. Neither he nor his aides had prepared a thought-through strategy for so mighty an enterprise as overthrowing the Board Chairman.

2. Vision of the Walls

Now, the Board Chairman had been at his business for several political lifetimes. He had also learned to compensate for his cold personality by calculating as far ahead as a methodical brain could envision.

Widely believed to be a man without humor, he liked to execute bold "jugular-cutting strokes"—a favorite phrase of his —as occurred the day that the Evangelist's credentials committee decided that the Baron of Daley, one of the largest fiefdoms in the realm, was too practical to be included in the march on the Castle. That same day the Board Chairman worked until midnight signing contracts for the construction of new barges and galleys at more generous subsidy rates than would have been legal had the contract been signed the following day.

This action the Board Chairman caused to be publicized widely in the newspapers that still circulated between the Castles and the Plains.

Tidings had reached him that crops had failed and there might even be famine in the Lands of the Red Barbarians, with whom he had engaged in lifelong strife.

In another political season the Board Chairman might have chosen to harass the Red Lands, but being under attack at home, the Board Chairman decided the time had come to declare peace with the Reds, while simultaneously selling them the wheat and corn that was surplus among the serfs, tenants, and corporate estates. This would also make possible reductions in the patrols of soldiers that ringed the Lands of the Reds—an issue which the Evangelist had been denouncing as needless empire-watching.

This wheat and corn would have to be loaded by short-shoremen onto galleys operating under his feudal flag, which called for higher than prevailing rates of pay.

The whole operation would increase the size of the feudal deficit, about which the Board Chairman lamented publicly at least once each week while increasing it daily. Still, he judged that an extra billion or two could be covered as long as the price of bread and meat did not rise until after the voting.

Many were the other stratagems that the Board Chairman mixed into his bag of "tricks and treats." But the decisive action, which led to his crushing victory over the Evangelist, was actually inspired by the troubled mood of the people in his realm.

For several years every part of his domain had been rocked by diverse disruptions, so much so that many wives and maidens feared to walk beyond the Castle walls after dark, and the price of a police dog rose almost as high as fees for psychiatrists.

There had been a dramatic increase in the numbers of eighteen-year-olds, most of whom refused to be warriors, and who made such demands as that curfews be abolished and drawbridges remain lowered at all hours. The unrest had also spread to many a knight's "fair lady," who formed a movement protesting against being looked upon as mere tournament objects for whose favor the knights jousted to be acclaimed with chauvinistic applause.

With the very foundations of knight-errantry under attack, the Board Chairman decided upon drastic action.

And so, once upon a prime time, it came to pass that the Board Chairman appeared on the widest screen to tell his people of a vision that had come to him of how law and order and knightly values would be restored to the land.

In this vision the Board Chairman had been told that the people had become too agitated with one another's burdens. By separating themselves from the tribulations of others, they would find a new tranquillity—yea, even repose.

What each person needed, the Board Chairman explained, was to acquire a private retreat walled off from the concerns of others which would shelter one from physical and psychological attack.

Therefore decreed the Board Chairman:

First, each individual soul should acquire a wall of his or her own.

Second, all should be governed by the new Knight's Ethic —every knight for himself.

Thenceforth all could live in harmony, divided from one another, separate but equal, be it in the suburbs or in the manor ghettos.

Afterwards, the more scholarly chroniclers were to marvel at the political genius of the Board Chairman in receiving such a vision at so troubled a time. One hailed it as worthy of comparison with an earlier decree of the Board Chairman that all men who wanted to be famous should arrange to be born on a holiday, since that would be good for weekend business.

Some Castle-watchers thought the vision of the walls simply reflected the many rebuffs and defeats the Board Chairman had suffered as a younger man, which had taught him how much strength and security could be found in the privacy of one's own wall.

Other chroniclers insisted that so inspired a vision could come only from God, a mysterious Being who, during the setting third of the twentieth century, had somhow got lost in a computer along with countless complaints of overcharging.

Many came to believe that God was dead. The more faithful felt certain that the Day of Judgment would come, when God would emerge to render justice and the meek would inherit the refunds.

However the vision was born, a new coalition of walls came into being, embracing all the Baronies of Labor and Castles of Feudal Enterprise. Even such tough guild masters as Sir George of Meanie recognized that with the walls would come the power to regulate the entry of newcomers so that wages, profits, and prices would be kept high.

Verily, one could hardly list the many ways in which the Board Chairman put his vision of walls into being. But perhaps two actions are worth noting.

Some time earlier the Board Chairman had decreed "Let there be unemployment" among workers in feudal space and defense establishments. Discontent polls reported that many of these workers were muttering they might defect to the Plains.

It was widely known that the Evangelist proposed to reduce the spending on Castle walls so as to be able to expand peaceful enterprise. When the Evangelist issued this pronouncement, the Board Chairman ordered his budgeteers to increase the building of defense walls, as well as the production of catapults, spears, and lances, adding overtime pay and cost-plus allowances, even while the Evangelist was urging lower defense spending.

But the Board Chairman took even greater pride in one

other achievement. His predecessors had left in the Big White House what purported to be a wondrous spending and job-making machine, said to be the invention of a certain Lord Keynes from Merrie England.

This Lord Keynes had calculated that by stimulating the machine with certain powerful statistics one could put nearly everyone in the whole realm to work.

At first the Board Chairman had sniffed at this machine, since he was a champion of "free enterprise." But at odd hours in the night and in the privacy of his chambers he couldn't resist tinkering with this Keynesian machine. He then discovered powers in this machine that the original disciples of Keynes had overlooked—to wit, that whoever controlled the making of new jobs could wield enormous political advantage, particularly in a period of unemployment.

By shifting "priorities," as the language of the times went, one could direct new work into the crafts favored by those loyal to the Board Chairman, while reducing work activity in the pursuits which attracted the Evangelist's supporters.

By offering well-paying positions and the security of a guild wall, the Board Chairman reasoned that many youthful long-hairs would be induced to shear their hair and come into the Castles. Thus they would become staunch defenders of the system of walls, along with defense guards and other retainers. Teachers, nurses, and similarly misguided souls could persist in their idealism in the underfinanced cold.

Given such developments, the "ins" would indeed outnumber the "outs," and the Board Chairman happily calculated he would carry the balloting in all fiefdoms in the land save two. These two had a special affection for a young lord, descended from a famous dynasty, who was thinking of challenging the Board Chairman sometime in the future. But that could be handled by the Board Chairman's successor, whoever he might be.

So ends this tale, at least as far as we know it now from the documents at hand. Unfortunately, we have not as yet found any record of what happened after the Board Chairman put his vision of walls into effect. Did the walls—real and psychological—which he decreed stand everlasting or collapse a few years later? Did some other champion of discontent arise who could organize the Plains of Anger more effectively than the Evangelist? What use did the Board Chairman make of the powers he gained by crushing the Evangelist? Were these powers employed to ease the problems of his people? To organize a crusade of feudal enterprise abroad?

These are questions that might be kept in mind as we return to Nixonland and examine what happened there in the critical political year of 1972.

Chapter *2*

Our First Total
Election

1. Nixon the Revolutionary

ONE TANTALIZING FACT might be noted about Richard Nixon's astonishing landslide sweep of forty-nine states—only fifteen months earlier he was sliding down to defeat.

During the spring and summer of 1971, even among Republicans, the comments voiced most frequently about him were, "He's too slow" and "He takes too long." In some precincts a third of the Republicans interviewed talked of voting against him. So turned off were most voters that even the announcement that he would visit Red China was shrugged off, despite the media acclaim.

Still, less than a year later and before Senator George McGovern was nominated, Nixon's re-election was assured.

How could the mood of the country have changed with such blitzkrieg speed? What happened in that historic year of decision that enabled Nixon to split apart the Democratic coalition, reshape much of the country's future, and push us into a new orbit of conflicts that seems likely to engage us for years to come?

Because the Democrats won control of both houses of Congress, netting two more Senate seats, Nixon's victory was widely downgraded as little more than a personal triumph over an "inept" and "extremist" opponent.

Certainly much of Nixon's sweep in carrying all but 128 of the 3,091 counties in the country must be attributed to the revulsions, angers, and bewilderments stirred by McGovern and his "new left" following. Still, to focus on McGovern's failings remains a distraction from the main event.

The main event was how, to win re-election, Nixon transformed the presidency, organizing it for political overkill and upsetting the constitutional balance with Congress and the electorate.

George McGovern and his youthful aides may have fancied themselves as the carriers of radical and sweeping change. The real political revolutionary was Richard Nixon.

What Nixon did was to organize and push through what can be described best as our first total election—total in the precise sense that virtually nothing was overlooked that might sway or alter voter feeling.

Other presidents—notably Franklin Roosevelt—employed all their reachable powers to gain re-election, but the process has never been carried through with such skill and absence of restraint as under Nixon.

The range of his activities was truly startling. The same combination of patient planning and economic concessions that made the trips to Moscow and Peking successful was also employed to woo labor-union leaders and split them from the Democratic Party.

Quotas on textile imports pleased the South Carolinians;

dropping requirements for black job openings gratified the construction unions; successive easing of the draft wore down much of the anti-war resistance. And yet such actions represented only one dimension of this total election.

Inescapably, this total election became an epic psychological contest—often psychological war—between the presidency and a deeply troubled electorate.

At stake was not simply how many votes might be picked up in November but how the future of the country was to be remade. In place of traditional campaigning, Nixon advanced or put into effect a whole series of controversial actions and policies which sought to commit the nation *beyond* the election—on defense spending, foreign policy, welfare, school busing, who was to make the jobs and who was to get them, who was to pay the taxes and who was to evade them.

Political writers like to think that Americans prefer to vote against rather than for a candidate. In 1972 many Americans were voting against other Americans.

Nixon did not create these divisions, but he did make them the terrain of political battle. In doing so, he seems to have structured them into continuing social conflicts—the racial polarization between the inner cities and suburbs, the budget clashes between demands for home and abroad, for defense and civilian spending needs, the gap between those secure "in" the economy and those who feel locked "out," the generation gap between the young and the old.

All of this was carried through outside the party system. Nixon did not need a Republican Party to win. McGovern had no Democratic Party. By election day not much was left to the voter but to ratify or reject what Nixon had done.

Such an all-or-nothing choice troubled many Americans. An Iowa farmer tried to explain the uneasiness that came with personal affluence and too much government power.

"We're living in a dictatorship," he grumbled. "They tell you what to plant, how much land you can use, what to keep idle. Then they pay you so much you can't afford to refuse what they want you to do."

Asked how he intended to vote, he replied, "Nixon. There's no choice between him and McGovern. But I'll be voting Democrat for Dick Clark for senator against Senator Miller, the Republican."

Jack Miller's defeat was one of the upsets of the election. An analysis of the vote shows that not only Democrats but many staunchly Republican counties and towns went for Clark.

The desire not to put all of one's eggs in Big Brother's basket transcended party lines.

What does total politics mean to a democracy like ours? In telling that story, this narrative concentrates on the domestic impact of the election, more particularly on three decisive battles of voter opinion—over race, the war, and Nixon's seizure of the economy—but also on a new technique for agitating and manipulating discontent and on Nixon's effort to spread the ideological creed of economic individualism in place of the old New Deal philosophy.

All five of these engagements have been intensified in Nixon's second term.

To capsule each:

1. *The Battle of Benign Neglect* / Rarely agitated openly in the formal campaign, the racial conflict brought the sharpest vote divisions in the country. In eight cities checked, typical black precincts went 85 to 95 percent for McGovern, although the turnout was about 20 percent lower than in 1968.

Nixon's heaviest gains over 1968 came in capturing almost the whole of the white South and in the racially polarized

northern cities and suburbs. The voters in these areas saw
Nixon committed to ending school busing and racial job quotas
and to minimizing government pressures on behalf of the
blacks.

Issue for the future: How far would this trend be pressed?
Would racial problems be pushed out of national politics, to
be left to states and localities? And what if ignoring racial
troubles only aggravates them?

2. *From Vietnam "with Honor"* / As late as the summer
of 1971, the national mood still was dominated by two desires
—"to get out of Vietnam" and "to take care of our own
problems." North Vietnam's Easter offensive and Nixon's
retaliatory bombing abruptly escalated public emotions to a
climax. Mining Haiphong Harbor brought Nixon the voter
shifts that assured his re-election—long before McGovern was
nominated—and also the voter support to stay in Vietnam
until after the election.

Issue for the future: Can any restraint be established on
the president's ability to plunge the nation into another war?
To commit us abroad on economic issues?

3. *The Targeting of Discontent* / Here we probe one of
the major mysteries of the election. Given the range and intensity of disgruntlement in the nation, one might have expected
the President to be turned out of office. Why did the Democrats lose this contest to manipulate and target these discontents?

Nixon did get a powerful assist from that master mechanic of discontent, George Wallace; still, the competition
really turned on two conflicting approaches toward government. With continued inflation, mounting taxes, and an uneven economic recovery, it proved easier to encourage each
individual voter to scramble for his own selfish interest than

to devise a program for sharing the burdens equitably by all.

Also contributing to the outcome were economic changes still not fully felt, such as:

The new political power of business as the maker of jobs.

The demoralizing expectation that inflation will be perpetual.

The rise of a military-industrial job complex—almost a second economy—directly responsive to the manipulations of the White House.

Issue for the future: Who really holds power in a government that agitates against "government" and against taxes?

4. *The Ideological Crusade* / Here the aim, not yet won, was to re-establish a modernized version of William McKinley's selfish individualism as the dominant domestic creed. The glitter in this ideology lies not in the ring of "traditional values" but in the fact that "individualism" enables voters to turn their backs on unsought or out-of-hand burdens—to break free, in short, from an overloaded sense of social responsibility.

As we will see, individualism generates its own competitive pressures to pass on to others all burdens and costs, even to pushing some people, issues, or problems out of sight. One such casualty was the family-assistance welfare plan that Nixon once so proudly hailed.

At the election's end the "anti-government" drive was still drawing most of its fuel from racial antagonisms; also, many anti-taxers wanted neither austerity nor discipline but just more.

Issue for the future: Can social responsibility and selfish individualism be reconciled?

5. *The Seizure of the Economy* / Unemployment, supposedly the strongest single Democratic advantage, was turned

into a Nixon asset. This was done not simply by adopting record-sized Keynesian deficits to stimulate prosperity.

"Reorder our priorities" had been the cry of Democrats and various citizen groups like Common Cause for years. Nixon took hold of the economy and set his own priorities, which favored defense, manufacturing, and business quite heavily, and restricted funds for fields like ecology, teaching, social services, and public employment generally.

The political importance of this choice of priorities was largely overlooked during the campaign. But when one examined the remarkably direct impact on many voters, particularly first voters, the critical significance of Nixon's control of the economy became evident.

Wherever they were interviewed, on campuses, at high schools, or in typical neighborhoods, the same psychological sorting process between the "ins" and "outs" could be seen.

It in fact, turned out to be quite like the division organized by the Board Chairman in our tale of modern feudalism.

Those youths and adults in the parts of the economy favored by economic expansion became defenders of Nixon's policies and of the system. McGovern sympathizers were almost always hard pressed economically or wanted to work in fields which fared poorly or were locked out under Nixon's job-making and spending priorities.

How the economy was structured, in short, was how their voting was structured. Or was it that the President's economic priorities had been set to appeal to those voters who could be expected to support Nixon and to cold-shoulder those most likely to favor McGovern?

Issue for the future: Should any president have the right to determine the economic priorities of the country, and use them for political purposes?

It is against this backdrop of total politics that the struggle between Congress and the President should be viewed. The stakes of the constitutional issue are not to be measured by the funds being impounded by the President. The spending powers of Congress, along with actions such as pressing the Watergate investigation, are among the powers still left through which Congress can restrain or balance the sweeping changes the President is pressing to restructure our government, our economy, the whole of society.

Young voters constitute a kind of "tracer" generation through which the effects of this struggle can be watched. Each year over the next nine years something like four million additional youths will be entering the labor market.

Are they to be required to shape up or else—as happened in 1972?

Or will their work and career opportunities be widened to fit their strivings and the needs of the country?

Some "hard-liners," of course, would use the economy as a means of disciplining young people and toughening their character.

The President himself apparently shares this view. At least, that was the implication in his much publicized interview for post-election use with Garnett D. Horner of the Washington *Star-News*, which linked Nixon's economic thinking with a vow to end "the whole era of permissiveness" and to "nurture a new feeling of responsibility . . . a new feeling of self-discipline."

Any thought that the economy can be employed to spank sense into the nation's youth is a managerial delusion. The vast majority of youths I have interviewed are not young radicals but are searching for useful and purposeful work.

To use the economy to force young people to accept the political views of those in power invites a lasting social cleavage instead of the reconciliation the country wants.

As I read the President's *Star-News* interview, I was re-
minded of a senior at Palisades High School in Bucks County,
Pennsylvania, who had been interviewed two days before the
election.

She had impressed me by her determination to become
a nurse against great difficulties. Her father, now fifty-eight,
had been laid off and was troubled about how he would live
when he was forced to retire. She was on her own.

When I went over the notes of her interview, it seemed
that here was someone who would be a sure winner in any Miss
Work Ethic contest. Yet she and her parents favored George
McGovern.

Here are some excerpts from her interview:

I always read the economic parts of the paper cause that's what
I worry about—there's too much unemployment.

I'd like to go to nursing school, but I have to put myself through
and I've had a hard time getting a job. I know so many people who've
been out of work. My father was laid off from his construction job
for twelve weeks this year.

I'm working as a nurse's aide now on Sundays. I tried at so many
hospitals before I got this, it was really bad. I applied to at least
thirty-five places—stores and hospitals, just everything. I went to
Allentown and Bethlehem and Quakertown.

I've saved enough money to get through my first year of nursing
school from what I made on after-school jobs, but I need more money
to get through nursing school. Last summer I got a job in a nursing
home, but the state came in and told them they had to cut back on
their budget. They kept the older workers and let the young people
go. Young people don't have a chance.

Even this setback didn't stop her job-hunting. She continued:

I tried all summer to find something because I really need that
money. I had good references from school and I make good grades,
but there was no work. . . . My father told me if I had the right
attitude and kept on trying, eventually I'd find a job.

But my father was looking for work at the same time. He went out every day. It made me think if it's so hard for my father to find work with his experience, then people like me who don't have a lot of experience, we have no chance at all.

The problems of young women like this one are now being shrugged off.

If this attitude persists, some part of the new "entry generation" will be turned into psychological left-outs.

2. "Ratification by the Manipulated"

Most basic college texts used in government courses describe our American democracy as "government by the consent of the governed." The question should now be added: Are we becoming a "government by the ratification of the manipulated"?

That query was suggested by my efforts to trace through the impact upon voters across the country of the many manipulations being tried by Washington. Which did the voters respond to? Which did they reject? Can a total politics be reconciled with our democratic habits?

This interviewing left one over-all conclusion: that we have been plunged deep into an era of presidential management of our society. Whole segments of the nation face a decade or more of economic squeeze-out, reflecting how job opportunities and the effects of chronic inflation both at home and abroad are manipulated.

Of the imposing array of powers employed by Nixon, the economic ones had the most dramatic impact on the voting. They directly reshaped the sense of self-interest of many individual voters; economic feelings also spilled over into attitudes on the war and racial conflicts.

Many of those economic powers were lodged in the presidency as part of the Keynesian revolution in economic thinking by which the government took on the responsibility of managing the economy. When that was done, with the tax cut of 1964, the man in the White House automatically became not just the president visualized in the Constitution but a president-manager, Lyndon Johnson being our first president-manager and Nixon the second.

The personalities of these two men differ appreciably. Still, as president-managers, both men were able to win landslide victories by making their opponents appear intent upon bringing down the whole system. Both presidents also were agitators of domestic discontent, albeit on different sides of the taxpayer barricades. Both weakened the party system and may have intensified the divisions inside the country.

Both also employed the federal budget as an ideological weapon to rearrange the pattern of economic conflict in the country and overcommit the future.

Johnson, for his part, inaugurated a dramatic expansion of spending for the public sector, with his unprecedented array of Great Society programs, from Medicare to increased aid to education, the poverty program, community action, added library funds, and so on. The political reasoning at the time was that the expectations aroused by each of these programs would create constituencies of voters who would resist future efforts to cut back on these funds.

In cutting down and ending many of these programs, Nixon has also been trying to build voter constituencies that would be beholden to his cause, made loyal by tax reductions and increased private spending and economic expansion abroad. To justify his expansion of the private sector, he has agitated as zealously against "government" as Johnson did against poverty.

Some Johnson programs were hastily contrived, as were some of Nixon's budget reductions. One irony of the enactment of the Great Society legislation was that it failed to anticipate the urban riots that were to explode in Watts within the year.

The "reforms" that Nixon is pressing to expand the private sector seem directed more to the politics of the past than to meeting the new problems tumbling in on us, such as the dollar and energy crises.

Several other observations might be noted about the political consequences of Keynesian economics. As a result, economics are becoming more political and psychological in their impact upon both the voters and our leaders. Restraint on the part of president-managers is apparently discouraged; they may even be encouraged to become gamblers, driven to overreach.

The Keynesian revolution also threatens to undermine what I have always regarded as the great strength of the American democracy: that we have not been ideological people but have been eminently practical, asking not how things are done but does it work.

The last election demonstrated, though, that our sense of pragmatism and self-interest can be manipulated and exploited. The Keynesian process also enables a president-manager to appear to perform wonders—for a time.

I recall the strange mood of euphoria that swept the country right after Johnson's landslide victory over Barry Goldwater. The reduction in federal taxes had left a general feeling that no one had to pay for any of the new government programs being enacted. Johnson seemed invincible, as a one-man government, until he overreached by plunging into the Vietnam war.

The ability to employ Keynesian deficits to whip up an economic boom and a crushing landslide is a stormy power. For Nixon's re-election, the money supply was boosted 8 percent and industrial production rose 11 percent, but imports jumped

25 percent, swelling the 1972 trade deficit to $6.8 billion, more than double what it was a year earlier.

Landslides can miseducate presidents. A politician who has swept the country assumes that he holds the confidence of the people. His aides may believe they have discovered the perfect formulas for successful manipulation. Or the victor may reason more crudely, "While I have the power I'll just push my political luck as far as I can and really remake the country the way it ought to be."

Self-restraint has never characterized the American politician or the American people generally. In fact, self-restraint seems the most un-American quality. Our Constitution, with its theory of colliding powers, encourages an optimistic game plan—that a president can run with the ball until he is tackled. What if the resistance cannot find effective political expression? Or takes too long to appear?

In this connection, it would be well to contrast the coalition that Nixon seems to be putting together with the old New Deal coalition which established the Democrats as the normal majority party in the country.

3. That "Nixon Coalition"

Twenty years ago, in *The Future of American Politics*, I wrote the story of how the Roosevelt coalition came into being and why it was able to reconcile and compromise the country's conflicts for so long.

One critical reason may well have been an accident of history, in the Solid South's being so Democratic.

Having suffered from a poverty of opportunity after the Civil War, Southerners found military careers particularly attractive. There developed a tradition of patriotism and concern for national defense which insured southern political support for every war president—for Franklin Roosevelt when he was troubled by midwestern isolationists during the Second World War, and for Nixon during the Vietnam conflict.

Within the New Deal coalition, the South, being more conservative, restrained northern liberal tendencies. Since Democratic presidents had to deal with Republican heads of business, this also tempered economic policies. The net result was moderate-paced change accompanied by a growing sense of social responsibility among businessmen.

From where within the "new Nixon majority" will similar restraints come?

As a newcomer element in the Republican Party, the South is likely to shed its old restraining role and become a force for sharpening conflict. Most southern Republicans and George Wallace supporters whom I have interviewed seem driven by the same competitive economic individualism and harsh "work ethic" that Nixon eulogizes.

A good part of the Republican appeal in the South has been developed by linking anti-government economics with racial resentments.

The dynamics of coalition conflict being what they are, the old-timer, more "liberal" urban Republicans may find themselves driven out of their party—a process that may have already begun in some New England areas where Nixon lost strength from 1968.

As for business, it has become the carrier of technological and political revolution. This is restoring business to its pre–New Deal dominance. With more than $86 billion in foreign investment, American-based multinational firms now thrive astride national boundaries. Here at home business has gained a new job-making prestige, often through tax incentives and subsidies. Balancing our economic interests at home and abroad has become one crisis after another.

In battling with Congress, Nixon invokes the separation

of powers, even while the separation between government and business becomes ever more difficult to find.

A basic, perhaps tragic contradiction is already embedded in the "Nixon majority." Its policies are directed largely to giving business a third leg with which to spread, but many of the dislocations thus kicked up can be made manageable only by "that damned government" which Nixon rhetoric keeps attacking. It is part of this contradiction that a President who talks of "giving power back to the people" should be reaching out steadily for new powers.

Voters will continue to want at least two and perhaps more parties to make certain that Big Brother doesn't take their votes for granted. It is uncertain what functions will be left to the parties, and how much power they will have beyond nominating the candidate. There may be no "center" left in either party. Nixon, to repeat a point made earlier, did not need a Republican Party to win, nor can his administration be regarded as "party government" in any real sense.

Along with Dean Burnham and David Broder, I find that our party system has become unstable and erratic. In the seven presidential elections since Franklin Roosevelt's death—from 1948 through 1972—we have experienced three cliff-hangers, settled by barely 1 percent of the vote, and four landslides. No election has reflected a true balance of party strength.

In 1976 no president-manager will be running for re-election. Will a race of two new men bring another close election? Or can Nixon's second-term strategy change that prospect?

The key to his strategy seems to lie in laying down an "attack plan" embodying a whole orbit of conflicts into which Nixon wants to force the politics of the future.

The terrain and order of upcoming battle is mainly a continuation of the total politics of 1972. Nixon's proposed

1974 budget (how could anyone describe a budget of $279 billion as "austere"?) continues his agitations for a taxpayer revolt against public spending, which would transfer more power to the "private sector."

The social cuts in the budget were accompanied by increases in defense, certain to be attacked by the Democrats, which Nixon might welcome in hope of establishing the Republicans as the pro-defense and anti-isolationist party.

A promise of tuition aid for Catholic parents repeated Nixon's 1972 bid to the Catholics. The relaxation of Phase III wage and price controls and his "protectionist" talk of raising some tariffs were publicized as efforts to hold the labor support he drew in 1972.

Some budget reductions may have been advanced to test voter resistance: which social programs would be fought for, which would stir little support? Other threatened cuts could serve as bargaining ballast to exchange for support of measures the President would want most, such as funds for Vietnam reconstruction or trade legislation.

Still, the picture is there of Nixon and his aides trying to pin onto the Democratic donkey a whole fistful of labels—big spenders, big taxers, anti-defense, "isolationist," pro-welfare, pro-black, pro-amnesty. The hope, of course, is to split the Democratic opposition anew.

How anti-government are the American people? Much of the Nixon landslide was a vote against McGovern, often with misgivings about Nixon's policies. What were the people actually voting for? Let us examine the major battles of voter opinion that were fought in 1972. How much of the future is locked into place and how much of it is still up for change?

Chapter *3*

A Racial Turning Point

1. Terrain of Defeat

SOME BATTLES cannot be won because one side occupies terrain that is unassailable. That was the story of the racial conflict in the 1972 election, as far as the Democrats were concerned. Nor is any quick change in the psychological, territorial, or political features of that terrain in sight.

The unassailable racial stone wall behind which Nixon had dug in was built partly on open agitation for an end to school busing but even more so on his policy of studied neglect. "We haven't had riots since he's been in" or "He hasn't given in to them" typified the comments voiced most frequently by onetime supporters of George Wallace and Hubert Humphrey in explaining why they were shifting to Nixon.

This desire to "slow the blacks down" reflected several significant changes in racial feelings from the 1968 election.

Nearly always when interviewed about racial problems, people framed their replies in terms of the future, as if trying to determine the conditions on which whites and blacks could live both together and apart—in what combination.

In 1968, after three years of racial rioting, one of the stronger voter dreads was of new eruptions of mass riotings by blacks in the cities.

That dread seemed gone in 1972, although fears of crime, muggings, and robberies were greater; also, concerns over any advantages given to blacks over whites. Protests were voiced against job preferences. Agitations over welfare were stirred— not only by the tax burden but by resentments that persons on welfare were getting medical and other benefits for which workers had to pay.

Compared with 1968, the opposition to school busing had actually intensified in the North, but had declined somewhat in the South. There parents supported busing in the hope that "if we take care of the problem now, it will be a dead issue in ten years."

A thirty-nine-year-old Florida engineer felt, "Busing has been good for my son. He's resolved problems with colored kids."

An auto salesman in Columbia, South Carolina., said, "My wife's a teacher and the colored are bused to her school. She says they're very bright but haven't gotten a good education until now."

But the terrain of public feeling was harshened by two other influences. First, the busing conflict had become a tool of party realignment. The voters sensed that political leaders were ready to yield on the issue as a means of gaining power. Then, the white movement to the suburbs suggested that whites might be able to break free physically of black desegregation efforts inside the cities.

After the Reconstruction period the blacks were indeed

pushed out of the effective arena of politics. Those were the years in which the South wrote Jim Crow laws.

That history might repeat itself today would seem unbelievable. Still, the temptation to try to ignore racial problems was there, in the fact that the racial issue could give one party the majority power and that suburbanites might think they could, as some urged, "leave the cities to the blacks."

Far from creating a self-correcting situation, any determination to lock blacks out of the suburbs would aggravate our racial crisis.

Between 1960 and 1970, in the nation's fifteen largest urban centers, the number of jobs in the suburbs rose 44 percent, but dropped 7 percent in the central cities, as shown in a special analysis of 1970 Census data by Jack Rosenthal of the *New York Times*.

How polarization has intensified year by year can be seen in the voting returns. Nixon's 1972 sweep could be read in the 1968 presidential vote and even more clearly in the Democratic Senate defeats suffered in 1970 in Maryland, Tennessee, Virginia, and New York.

In Maryland, the votes that defeated Senator Joseph Tydings in 1970 were cast in the areas where George Wallace fared best in 1968.

Inside the city of Baltimore, the thirty-three precincts which voted 30 percent or more for Wallace gave Nixon only 26 percent in 1968. This climbed to 51 percent Republican for Tydings' opponent, Senator J. Glenn Beall, in 1970, and 70 percent for Nixon in 1972. The suburbs east of Baltimore which gave Nixon 35 percent in 1968 voted 59 percent Republican in 1970, and 74 percent Nixon in 1972.

The counties on Maryland's Eastern Shore, emotionally part of the Old South, went 47 percent for Nixon in 1968, 69 percent for Senator Beall in 1970, and 72 percent for Nixon in 1972.

In Tennessee, the terrain of past voting and history was even more deeply rutted.

Shelby County, which consists of Memphis and its suburbs, supplied nearly half the total state plurality by which Republican William Brock defeated Albert Gore. Every white precinct in the city went against Gore, but Humphrey in 1968 had also lost every white precinct, as had Frank Clement, who ran against Senator Howard Baker in 1966.

Nixon got only 32 percent of Shelby County's vote in 1968 (Wallace drew 33 percent); this climbed to 55 percent for Senator Brock in 1970, to 67 percent for Nixon in 1972.

In the Whitehaven section of Memphis, which has boomed with transplanted white Mississippians, the comparable figures are: 46 percent for Nixon in 1968, 82 percent for Brock in 1970, and 87 percent for Nixon in 1972.

The election of "moderate" governors in Florida, South Carolina, and Arkansas in 1970 led some Democratic leaders to hope that parts of the South might be held in 1972 on economic issues.

These hopes, though, ignored the dynamics of southern resistance to desegregation and to the national leadership of the Democratic Party. The goal of Nixon's southern strategy had been to unite the 1968 Wallace and Republican voters, and nothing that would contribute toward that end—from textile quotas for South Carolina to the nomination of two Southerners to the Supreme Court—was overlooked. The decision of the vast majority of Southerners to swing to Nixon was set long before McGovern was nominated.

As I wrote in *The Hidden Crisis in American Politics*, "After 1968 an alliance between the white South and northern urban dwellers had to be put down as politically possible."

2. *"The Catholic Church Is Misguided"*

"Detroit is the big test case for the nation on busing," remarked the wife of one auto worker living just north of the city in the suburb of Warren.

Here the issue was not busing alone but the drive to end integration altogether. For a time at least, in the early spring when economic angers were strong, the Democrats seemed to be holding down the political effects of busing. By summer, though, Democratic hopes had caved in.

The final tally showed a Nixon sweep of 64 percent of the vote in Warren, an impressive gain over the 26 percent he drew in 1968.

Back in 1952, Eisenhower won 36 percent of the 16,000 votes cast in Warren's seven voting precincts. By 1972, the presidential vote in the city's 111 voting precincts had quadrupled to 65,000.

Mainly auto workers, more than half of those interviewed had moved to Warren from Detroit, and their feelings were dominated by the thought that, having separated themselves from black people, they wanted to remain separate. Brought up were memories such as these:

"Our house on 6 Mile Road and John R was broken into three times." . . . "When the first colored family moved in, three white families moved out." . . . "The colored didn't take care of their places." . . . "There were fires and alarms every other night." . . . "There were street fights." . . . "The colored were rougher than whites." . . . "The schools were so bad, when my parents moved out here I got put back a grade." Many went on to state flatly that they wanted segregation.

Declared the wife of an Air Force pilot, "Integration won't happen in my lifetime and I hope not in my children's lifetime either."

Another mother remarked, "Integration is a lost cause.

The way kids are brought up today, if you're white, you're anti-colored, and if you're colored, you're anti-white. That's just the way it is."

A few persons conceded, "They can go to our school if they live in the neighborhood." Questioned further, they admitted, "only one colored family lives in Warren."

The thought of living in an integrated community seemed to have been pushed out of their minds.

Some even suggested, "If the colored want to live out here, they should move into one of the new subdivisions further out in the county. Decide ahead of time whether it'll be colored or white and then make it an all-colored subdivision. That way they could have their own school."

Although there was very little give racially, there was more on the political side. In the spring some who were angry about busing still talked of wanting a Democratic president.

"I'd keep my son home before sending him to Detroit," vowed the wife of a construction worker. "We bought our house to be close to the school. I went to school with them in Detroit, and I don't want my children bused back there."

But when asked if she wanted Nixon re-elected, she replied emphatically, "No way. Republicans hurt the little man and put him out of work. My husband was laid off five months this winter and seven months the year before. We had to send in unemployment checks for our our house payments.

"My brother couldn't find a job for two years," she went on, "so he enlisted and got sent to Vietnam. Now he's back and still has no job."

Similarly, the wife of a tool- and diemaker recalled that her husband had voted for Wallace in 1968, but now "our whole family feels we've got to get a Democrat in there."

Her husband, who had been laid off for six months, was still working irregularly.

"He needs thirty days work to get his hospitalization

paid," she explained. "When the company calls him back, they lay him off before he hits thirty days."

On school busing, she revealed, "Everybody's buying shotguns in Warren, in case the colored try to start anything. I'm a pretty good shot myself. I'm not gonna fire at 'em first, but I'll take my little girls to the basement. If the colored come in after us I'll shoot.

"My husband's gonna teach 'em judo when they're four years old," she added.

By July, though, Nixon had been to Russia—and McGovern to Miami. More important, the workers were better off financially, anti-busing resentments were surfacing, and a strong turn to Nixon was under way.

In March, a twenty-seven-year-old forklift driver had complained, "The only thing keeping me working is my seniority." He was going for Wallace in the May primary, but if Wallace didn't get the nomination, he wanted "a Democrat against busing. The Democrats are for the working man."

Reinterviewed in July, he had gotten a raise and purchased a new Dodge Maxiwagon. Now racial feeling rather than economic uncertainty was determining his vote. He shrugged off the UAW's endorsement of McGovern, saying, "It makes no difference cause the union's all black."

If busing went through, he vowed, "I won't send my two kids to school. I'll get a private tutor. I'm paying taxes here, so why should I send my kids to school in Detroit to be with blacks? I've got to vote for the man who won't bus 'em."

How prosperity had weakened the hold of the Democratic Party could also be seen in a Catholic family.

The wife of a fifty-six-year-old Chrysler worker recalled proudly, "My grandfather was the first justice of the peace in Warren and my father was the first electrician."

No one in the family had ever voted Republican, but in

1972 "most of the votes in this house will be going Nixon's way. We decided a year ago."

She felt better off economically because "our house is paid for and we got central air conditioning this year."

Her husband was eligible for retirement, "but I think Frank will stay on a few more years. We have two children still in school, and if they want to go to college, he'll have to keep on working. We'll get $6,000 a year pension, but after state and fereral income tax, you only get $5,000 of it. I was shocked. Imagine taking all that tax from a retired person!"

"These taxes really gripe me," she said. "The way welfare is dished out, we need the CCC camps again. We need somebody to stop these giveaway programs; we've got to slow them down. And McGovern has this crazy scheme to give 'em even more.

"We don't go into the city any more ourselves, and I'm not having my children bused in there," she went on. "I have only two school-age kids left, and we can't afford to put them into Catholic school."

Her eighteen-year-old daughter, Linda, interjected, "The real reason is you don't like what the Church teaches any more."

Her mother agreed. "That, too. Plus we can't pay for tuition with Frank about to retire.

"Our good old cardinal at the church here," the mother continued, "he says to hell with whites. He talks about the 'affluent suburbs.' We're not so affluent. He asks us to give and give, and it all goes to the colored in the city.

"After Martin Luther King was killed, the Church was going on and on about minority groups. And I said, 'Wait a minute—I've eaten kosher and oriental and I get along with everybody, but this is going too far.' Our cardinal wanted one colored family on every block in Warren.

"The Catholic Church is misguided. It's all a bunch of screwball dramatics. When my girls were in high school, the church had 'em baking cakes to take into the inner city to dope addicts."

Linda interrupted, "They don't even teach about saints any more."

"Not even the Ten Commandments," added her mother.

Linda remarked, "I had a good course on witchcraft this year, though."

At that point, the oldest daughter, Donna, came home. She was elated to find a letter from her boy friend at National Guard summer camp. Still dressed in a neat white uniform, Donna had just completed a day's nursing duty as a student at an inner-city hospital where the patients were mainly black.

She had voted for Edmund Muskie in the Democratic primary and was now for McGovern. Although troubled about school busing, she wanted more integration, explaining, "If kids grow up together, we'd all get along better."

Significantly, the one McGovern voter in this family still had some ties with the central city, while the pro-Nixon voters had cut themselves free.

This psychological tie-in held with first voters generally. Those who pitched their vocations or careers to working on the problems of the cities stayed Democratic; those who wanted nothing to do with blacks favored Nixon.

During the 1960–70 decade, the number of jobs in Detroit's inner city dropped by 23 percent, while suburban jobs increased by 62 percent. The Warrenites interviewed realized that living in the suburbs put them close to where the employment was.

"Factories and insurance companies have left the inner city and moved to the suburbs," remarked a carpenter's wife who was shifting from Wallace to Nixon.

"I don't believe companies have any encouragement to stay in the city," she added. "They can't get the right kind of help there."

A retired Chrysler supervisor thought, "Detroit is going to the dogs. Business is moving out to the suburbs cause they're scared of their white women employees getting molested and raped."

If jobs inside the cities continue to move away, the terrain of racial conflict will change. Will it bring a realization that the problems of the cities and suburbs cannot be overcome separately? Or will it make both races more warlike?

3. "I Hate Nixon but . . ."

Inside the big cities the racial conflict has also become a territorial struggle, but here the terrain doesn't permit any sharp, white-black division.

The polarization has been a process of movement and neighborhood change, often resisted for as long as possible.

After the 1968 election I mapped George Wallace's vote precinct by precinct in fourteen northern cities. Each city mapped broke apart into territorial halves. On one side was a virtually solid black city still expanding to find new housing for its swelling numbers, and confronted on the other side by hostile white voters.

The zones of sorest tension—where Wallace drew the heaviest 1968 vote—were on the edge of Negro residential expansion, where the Black Cities on the move pressed against still largely white areas.

The political effects of this continued polarization can be seen in the table which follows. Each of the five cities listed experienced elections for mayor after 1968 which divided the vote along racial lines.

For each of the cities, the wards or assembly districts

which voted 70 percent or higher against the pro-Negro mayoral candidate are shown, along with their vote for president in 1968 and 1972. The pent-up tensions which dominated these mayoral elections exploded in gains for Nixon of 20 to 24 percentage points in 1972.

TABLE 1
Nixon's Gains in Anti-Negro Big City Wards

WARDS 70% + FOR ANTI-NEGRO MAYORAL CANDIDATE*	1968 % NIXON	1968 % WALLACE	1972 % NIXON
Philadelphia	36	14	60
Cleveland	31	18	53
Detroit	31	13	51
New York City	45	7	66
Newark	38	19	62

*In Philadelphia, districts 70%+ for Rizzo in 1971, in Cleveland, wards 70%+ for Perk in 1969; in Detroit, districts 70%+ for Gribbs in 1969, in New York City, comparable assembly districts 70%+ against Lindsay in 1969, in Newark; precincts 70%+ for Addonizzio in 1970.

The white voters in these cities are primarily so-called ethnics—first- and second-generation immigrants from Italy and Central Europe.

The conflict between blacks and Italo-Americans has been particularly sharp in cities like Newark, Cleveland, New York, and Philadelphia, where Frank Rizzo, who was elected mayor in 1971, campaigned for Nixon.

Italo-Americans, who like to live in the neighborhoods where their parents lived, seem more intent than other ethnics in resisting the residential expansion of the blacks. Many of them also compete with blacks for city jobs and other employment.

South Philadelphia, for example, has been on the edge of the "black city" for a full decade. A truck driver's wife, shifting from Wallace to Nixon, explained, "I voted for Rizzo because he keeps the colored in tack [intact].

"They're coming closer to us," she went on. "They're on Mifflin Street already, only two block away. People say they'll never get up this far, but I don't know. I don't want 'em around me."

Nixon drew only 25 percent of South Philadelphia's vote when he ran against John Kennedy in 1960; by 1968, his vote had risen to 41 percent; by 1972, to 61 percent. In none of these cities has the election of a black mayor or a white mayor made any decisive difference in dealing with the agonies of these cities. The problems remain far too acute.

This point may be worth some emphasis in view of the desire expressed by Southerners and suburbanites to push the racial issue out of effective national politics. The turmoil and problems of the inner city are not self-correcting. They will not be overcome by being ignored.

In New York City, the jagged line of black-white polarization was first drawn in the 1966 referendum that killed the civilian review board that had been set up by Mayor John Lindsay to hear cases of alleged police brutality. Gotham's voters have divided along this same line of racial polarization in every election since: in 1968, where Nixon fared best and worst; in Lindsay's re-election on a three-party split in 1969; and in the 1970 voting for senator and governor.

All of the fourteen assembly districts where Conservative Senator James Buckley drew a clear majority voted 70 percent or better in 1966 to kill the civilian review board; none gave Lindsay as much as a third of their vote in 1969.

Governor Nelson Rockefeller's showing followed the identical pattern of polarization, leaping 20 percent and more from his 1966 vote in the districts most heavily opposed to the review board and dropping in the districts which stuck with the board.

With each of these elections the polarization has become somewhat more intense and has spread through a wider area of New York, as the expanding numbers of blacks and Puerto Ricans have pressed into new neighborhoods.

By 1972 these tensions had reached into Queens, the city's main home-owning borough, and into middle-class Jewish neighborhoods, long the most "liberal" of all white Democrats and once the strongest supporters of civil rights movements.

Two Queens precincts, where I interviewed in earlier elections, more than doubled their Nixon vote.

"I hate Nixon," declared the wife of a thirty-two-old aviation administrator in the Union Turnpike section of Queens when interviewed in 1970. She still was voting Democratic for Senate then, but revealed, "I'd really like to see Buckley get in."

Reinterviewed in 1972, she was moving to Nixon. "I'm becoming more conservative," she explained. "I just don't automatically support anything liberal like I used to. Before my children got in school, I supported busing because that was the liberal thing to do. Now with my kids in school, I'm conservative.

"The one thing I like about Nixon is his intervention on the school busing problem," she went on. "Now maybe we can end these busing programs altogether.

"The colored want privileges the whites don't have," she added. "They get jobs just because they're black. Sometimes on welfare you get more than when you work. The government should start work projects like during the war."

A civil engineer's wife protested in 1970, "We pay taxes and work very hard. Yet we're afraid to walk the streets. We need law and order."

Although sticking Democratic for Sena.e, she confessed, "If Buckley weren't a Conservative, I'd go .ur him."

By 1972, she was leaning to Nixon, explaining, "Some of the moves these liberals make are foolish. This busing issue has caused nothing but trouble."

She also attacked McGovern's war stand because "we're the most powerful country and shouldn't be humiliated like this. McGovern would name Jane Fonda our Secretary of Defense."

The second Queens precinct visited was in Forest Hills, where the city had proposed erecting a low-income housing project, which evoked intense opposition.

"We're prisoners in our own homes," protested a salesman and his wife who had never voted for a Republican but who were shifting to Nixon in 1972. "We're afraid to walk out of our house after dark. Criminals in this country have more rights than innocent people locked up in their homes. Bring back the electric chair. They go to jail and the government supports them with our taxes."

"Minorities are getting everything now, and they're squeezing out the middle class," the husband complained. "We lived in a little flat in Brownsville; we were poor, but we worked our way up and never asked for help. People on relief want everything for nothing and won't work for it."

"I'm sorry, but I'm tired of it," his wife added. "I don't want to hear about their problems any more."

In addition to racial feelings, by summertime Jewish voters were being split by the many factors that were affecting other voters in the country—indignation over taxes, inflation, and welfare, a lessened concern over the war, and George McGovern himself. The role of Israel seemed important earlier in the campaign but, despite the publicity, was not the principal influence in the Nixon vote gain.

Our interviewing, in fact, revealed more torment and

indecision among Jews than in any other voting group in the nation. Largely, this reflected a deep reluctance to leave the Democratic Party and a dislike for both candidates.

Those who favored Nixon explained, "It's not that I trust Nixon, but you can't believe anything McGovern says."

Those sticking with McGovern reversed the phrasing to say, "I can't stand McGovern, but I hate Nixon more."

Among well-to-do Jews, in suburbs like Scarsdale, economics were the dominant factor prompting their pro-Nixon turn.

Mainly business executives, Wall Street brokers, doctors, and the like, no other element in the country had voted as steadily Democratic in the past at so high a level of economic affluence.

Recalled one textile importer, "I thought McGovern must be nuts when he said we can't leave our money to our kids."

Others felt, "Nixon hasn't been bad for our business" or "He hasn't hurt us."

Other affluent families were caught in the curious ambivalence between a traditional sympathy for liberal causes and the practical fear of McGovern's tax plans.

A dentist's daughter explained, "My eighteen-year-old brother is very liberal; he worked for the migrant farm workers for a while. But my father is in a high tax bracket; he makes over $50,000 a year. My brother is afraid that under McGovern my father would lose everything he's worked for."

Among Jews shifting to Nixon, four of every five said they thought blacks were pushing too fast.

A liquor salesman's wife protested:

"McGovern's welfare scheme is outrageous. I don't worry about the submerged third, the so-called poor minorities, because they're taken care of on relief.

"And I don't worry about the rich because they're taken care of very well by Nixon. It's the middle class that I worry about."

This lament, that the "middle man is being squeezed from top to bottom," was bewailed across the whole country. McGovern staffers told newsmen these outcries were evidence of "alienation," ignoring the fact that neither McGovern nor any other New Deal Democrat has been able to appeal to voters hostile to both the rich and the poor, who are thought of now as mainly black.

Given this squeeze, the general effect was to turn middle-class angers against the blacks.

For a time the likelihood that the Jews would break for Nixon received more publicity than almost any other aspect of the election. Some Nixon advocates argued that Jews were turning conservative, advancing elaborate reasons why.

The split among the Jews does indeed indicate that the loyalties and antagonisms of the Roosevelt period have lost force. Still, one characteristic that has distinguished Jewish voting is a high sense of social responsibility. Currently, they share a general feeling that too much has been loaded onto that social responsibility, on what government can or should do. By temperament, though, most Jews are not likely to accept the anti-government ideology of selfish individualism that Nixon has advanced.

In this regard, their feelings would run counter to recent developments in the South.

4. The Mechanization of the Baptists

Considering the agitation over ethnic groups, surprisingly little attention has been paid to the one ethnic element that is currently having the most explosive political impact on the country—the white Southern Baptists.

The same mechanization of southern agriculture which displaced millions of blacks from the land into the northern cities also moved the sons and daughters of once despised "rednecks" cityward. In the process they found their political voice in George Wallace and—the largest single denomination in the South—may well have emerged holding the balance of voting power in the South and perhaps in the whole country.

Nixon's speeches, in fact, seemed designed to appeal to the traits which characterize Baptists—an ingrained individualism, suspicions of government, and resentment of taxes.

Childhood memories of poverty have also given them a hungry drive for material gain—often both husbands and wives work—and scornful contempt for blacks on welfare.

Some of these traits are shared by white Southerners generally; still, much of the ingrained individualism reflects their Baptist upbringing. Back in 1936, many Baptist ministers refused to give information to the Census Bureau for the religious census it was carrying out. Each Baptist church is independent—there is no Baptist church hierarchy—and anyone who feels the call to preach can ordain himself a minister.

"Ours is not a fancy religion like Catholic," explained a Virginia construction worker. "It's just straight from the Bible and no nonsense."

The wife of a polymer operator described herself as "independent Baptist," explaining, "The preacher teaches straight from the Bible. He doesn't make up his own sermon. He teaches what's right and what's wrong—not what you 'ought' to and 'ought not' to do like in other churches."

Baptists generally do not hold society responsible for man's failings, but believe that each man must find personal salvation by mastering his own inner soul and coming to know Jesus personally. They seem less concerned with changing society than with changing oneself.

In their attitude toward social responsibility, in fact, Baptists seem virtually opposite to the Jews, whose political attitudes are structured by a highly active social conscience.

Jews and Baptists—both of whom broke for Nixon—can be watched in the future as the carrier elements of the conflict between social responsibility and selfish individualism that is being fought out in this country.

Although many are still farmers, more and more Baptists are expanding into the new middle class of factory and white-collar workers. They have boats and two cars in their yards, air conditioning, and color TV, but not too many books.

This affluence of recent years is an important political divider between two generations of Baptists—the older ones who received their immersion during the Depression and the younger ones whose immersion took place during the civil-rights years.

A father and son I interviewed in Memphis in 1970 capsuled this generational difference.

They were working on the son's car, a 1968 Chevy. Corinth, Mississippi, had been their home, but after World War II they had come to Memphis as part of a migration of both whites and blacks, which led to Memphis's being called "the largest city in Mississippi."

Both father and son voted for Wallace in 1968. The father was not going to vote in the 1970 Senate race. "I don't want Gore and I can't vote Republican." He explained, "I remember when Hoover was president you couldn't get work for a dollar a day.

"Roosevelt came in. He closed the banks and opened the work."

The son broke in, "Those days are gone. I came up here in 1948, and I've worked steady, never lost a day's pay." He and his wife were voting for Brock "not because he's a Republican but the Democrats have become a nigger party. We white folk need a party of our own."

He added belligerently, "No one's going to make me bus my girl to a colored school."

This combination of racial angers stimulated by economic progress seems to be the key force in southern readiness and even eagerness for a new political party.

Memories that "the Democrats are better" for workers and farmers have not been completely uprooted. In labor precincts in cities like Greensboro, North Carolina, Norfolk, Virginia, and Houston, Texas, a third of Wallace's 1968 vote stuck with McGovern.

Oil-refinery and aerospace workers in Houston and Fort Worth shook their heads vigorously at the suggestion that John Connally might run for president; pro-business Texans, though, were delighted at the prospect.

For southern workers in political transition, Wallace has been the ideal spokesman. His direct-talking attacks on the establishment chime neatly with a favorite theme in Baptist sermons, that "higher-ups" are not as close to the truth as the ordinary man.

Through his anti-tax agitation, Wallace managed to merge the anti-government economics of Republican businessmen with the anti-government racial resentments of the workers. In 1972, Wallace supporters often cast heavier pro-Nixon margins than old-time Republicans did.

The Broad Rock section of Richmond, Virginia, where Wallace got 40 percent in 1968, gave Nixon 92 percent in 1972. The prevailing feeling was voiced by the wife of a casket salesman, who said, "The only issue I follow is busing."

To her that issue meant "the government wants to tell us what to do with our children. But I'll raise them the way I want to."

So intense was this anti-government feeling that many parents balked at proposals that federal funds be given to private segregated schools, or even that tuition grants be made to parents.

The feeling ran:

"I wouldn't be obligated to the government for anything."

"The government just wants a toe hold on us to do what they want with us. There's no telling what they'd do. I don't trust 'em."

Some Richmond families had taken their children out of public school and put them in a church school.

"Now my children get more religion," explained an Allied Chemical workers' wife. "They say the Lord's Prayer at the beginning of each day. I could never see why they took prayer out of the schools. Even in kindergarten they teach them Bible verses"

On a 1970 trip to Broad Rock, the school integration push had angered many into protesting that "Nixon is two-faced" and "a damned Republican pawn," or "I heard him say he was against busing, but he didn't do what he promised."

At that time, most workers interviewed were voting for Senator Harry F. Byrd, Jr., despite a long family tradition of anti-Byrd feeling.

One city worker recalled that when his father sold the family farm in 1954 and moved to Richmond, "I was only fourteen and I had to learn how to wear shoes. The guys used to kid me cause I talked funny."

A Wallace voter in 1968, he had never voted for Byrd because "I'll never forget when Byrd's daddy said that the working man is only worth fifty cents a day and a pair of overalls."

But in 1970 he shifted to Byrd because "he's maddest of

all against the busing." In 1972 this city worker went for Nixon.

A forty-eight-year-old construction worker, strong for Wallace when interviewed in 1968, recalled, "My daddy always said a workin' man can't vote for no Byrd."

By 1970 he felt, "Byrd don't seem too much against the workin' man like before. I know this much about him—he's anti-Negro and that's all I need to know."

To sum up, the forces of racial polarization still are pushing strongly for Republican realignment and could bring a bolt of the more anti-Negro Democrats.

The nomination of someone like Senator Edward Kennedy would electrify the most dispirited black voters and swell their turnout. In Freeport, Long Island, the wife of a sanitation engineer expressed indifferent support for McGovern. When asked about Kennedy, she lifted her head and replied, "A Kennedy will always be great in the black man's eyes. Without Kennedy, every black man believes we wouldn't be where we are now."

But one man's charisma can be another man's poison. Many white Democrats say, "All this racial trouble started with the Kennedys," or "I'd never vote for a Kennedy."

Southerners are not likely to quit the Democratic Party altogether; it remains too valuable a political property. The South may try to capture the Democratic Party, perhaps in league with mayors of racially troubled cities. A paralyzing party battle is possible in 1976.

By now, though, this much seems clear—if the Democrats are to regain the White House, they will have to do so on the weight of other than racial issues; yet the economic appeal of the Democrats is also being shaken.

Chapter *4*

The Politics
of Discontent

1. Every Man for Himself

BORN OF THE GREAT DEPRESSION in the 1930s, the Democratic coalition has always drawn new vigor from economic distress. Only two years after Eisenhower's second landslide, the recession of 1958, which chilled and fevered the country with both unemployment and inflation, brought a historic Democratic sweep of 283 seats in the House and 64 in the Senate.

This reassertion of the Democratic economic appeal, spilling over into 1960, helped John F. Kennedy become the first Catholic president.

The opening of the 1972 campaign stirred comeback hopes among the more optimistic Democrats. Never a popular figure, Richard Nixon was still regarded with special hostility by some Democratic voting groups. The scope and intensity of discontent in the country was astonishing—an unsettled war, unemployment, rising prices, mounting taxes, and climbing welfare loads, school busing, retirement fears. Virtually everyone interviewed had some grievance.

Yet it was just this sheer profusion of dissatisfaction that was to overwhelm the Democrats. No possible "program" could unify these discontents.

During the early months of 1972, my own interviewing revealed that most voters felt caught up in the grip of an economic squeeze-out which was fragmenting and dividing the country politically.

Instead of uniting their angers, the uneven, erratic recovery and persistent inflation were forcing each individual to scramble for his own self-interest, pushing off what burdens he could onto someone else.

Nixon was losing some of his 1968 supporters because of new job layoffs and protests that "he froze my wages but not prices." The 5.5 percent wage guideline was often contrasted with a "30 percent jump in hospitalization" or a "10 percent raise in utilities," or high auto-insurance boosts.

The President's drive for increased worker productivity also hurt him politically, since it led many companies to try to force older workers into early retirement.

But there were mixed voter effects from the "populist" agitation against taxes that Wallace sparked and which dominated the Democratic primaries.

Many workers grumbled, "The big boys have all the tax loopholes and the people have none." But in the economic squeeze-out going on, every use of government was becoming a tax issue. And some uses of government split Democratic voter feeling.

Welfare brought protests that "people on relief are crushing the middle class." This anti-welfare grievance was targeted against every Democrat but Wallace, and helped Nixon through the whole campaign.

Other tax angers were directed at governors of both parties—Richard Ogilvie, a Republican in Illinois, and Democrat Milton Shapp of Pennsylvania—both of whom had initiated new state taxes. When the Susquehanna River flooded, a paper-mill worker in West York remarked, "I don't like to see nobody get hurt, but I was so happy when the governor's mansion got flooded and they had to take Shapp out in a boat."

One other factor is worth emphasizing—that many of the grievances being aired were exaggerated and did not reflect real hardship.

It seemed, in fact, that the more people had financially —this was particularly true of voters shifting to Nixon—the stronger was their drive for still more gain and the louder their outcries against "government." The Wallace-Nixon agitations against taxes encouraged gripes which didn't really exist.

Here are a few varied examples:

A zoning examiner had gotten a new job which paid $3,000 more a year. Still his wife protested, "We're worse off now." In explaining how come, she revealed that in her husband's new job deductions were being taken for (a) life insurance, (b) a retirement pension, and (c) hospitalization, which the old job didn't provide for. "We had more take-home pay," she explained, "when they didn't take out for all that."

In Cocoa Beach, Florida, a woman who already owned two houses complained that she couldn't afford to buy still more property at Cape Kennedy.

The wife of an auto worker protested, "Taxes on our property have leaped in twenty-two years from $24 to $600 a year." In that twenty-two-year period, though, this couple had paid off the mortgage fully, while the value of their house had risen by $30,000. Still she argued, "Older people shouldn't have to pay property taxes."

One homeowner who complained, "We can't make ends meet," had a new 1972 Dodge Van in her driveway. The price tag was $6,047.92.

In trying to target these churning discontents against Nixon, the Democratic candidates labored under two further handicaps. They failed to appreciate how anti-government was the thrust of Wallace's "populism" and how it undermined the whole New Deal philosophy of using government in a responsible way.

Then, key Democratic leaders had decided, perhaps through wishful thinking, that the election would turn on the issue of "confidence"—that "people will vote for the man they trust."

This judgment overlooked the first fact of voter psychology, that when voters look at or listen to a candidate, they try to project into him their own emotions, interests, and beliefs.

To the voter, charisma and credibility in a candidate are like seeing one's self in a mirror. No one running for president comes through separate from the stands that he takes on the more critical conflicts of the election.

Reinforcing this illusion in "credibility" as an effective issue was the polling being done for George McGovern by Pat Caddell, a Harvard graduate, who was reporting that voters generally were "alienated" and "turned off" by "all politicians" and could be won over by someone who was "free of the political image."

But what did "alienation" mean? Blacks were disgusted with government because they felt let down; southern whites because their kids were being bused to school with blacks.

The polling failed to follow through on how specific voter grievances were being targeted, which were directed for or against what candidates, which were aimed against other voters, and which were like arrows shot in the air to land I know not where.

My own methodology enables me to do that kind of interviewing. Since I base my election judgments on how and why voters are shifting from the past, I rely on relatively small numbers of intensive interviews, exploring each individual's feelings thoroughly, as a whole person. In precincts where I have interviewed in previous elections, I often talk to the same families.

In our questioning for the 1972 primaries we began by asking each voter how he or she felt about Richard Nixon. Did the voter want him re-elected? How had the person gone four years ago when Nixon, Hubert Humphrey, and George Wallace were running?

Only after I had determined where each voter stood in regard to the President did I move in with questions on the Democratic candidates in the primaries.

This order of questioning revealed that many persons who were voting in the Democratic primaries, including large numbers of 1968 George Wallace supporters, had already decided to vote for Nixon in November.

How people described themselves was often misleading. In Tampa a carpenter said, "I'm sixty years old and have been a union man all my life. The Republicans have never been for labor."

A few questions later, he disclosed that he owned two apartment houses and his strongest economic concern was the taxes paid on this property; also that he had already decided to vote for Nixon against "any Democrat other than Wallace."

Actually, two interrelated economic struggles were going on that spring:

Over jobs, with new layoffs still taking place, older workers were fighting to hold on to their jobs, while women and record numbers of young workers were trying to get into the labor market.

Over the effects of inflation, with everyone trying to cut rising costs—food, hospitalization, auto insurance, utilities, taxes.

Each of these struggles produced divided political feelings.

2. Squeeze-out: Two Economies

Sometimes whole communities were caught in this economic squeeze-out. The contrast between two areas was revealing—as with Cape Kennedy in Florida and Akron, Ohio.

At Cape Kennedy virtually everyone interviewed still recalled the "terrible space layoffs of 1969," the "wage bust" that followed when "we had to take salary cuts to keep our jobs." Many spoke of "three years with no wage increases while prices have kept going up," and of new job losses that threatened.

The wife of a Lockheed technician remarked, "Last week they laid off the man before my husband, and he's next."

In Akron, the squeeze-out complaints sounded much the same: "Our contract calls for a raise in August, but they want us to give it up." . . . "Three of my brothers and sisters have already moved to Florida because of factories leaving here." . . . "We bought our house two years ago and had to make the payments with unemployment checks." . . . "My husband just got called back, but they say more layoffs are coming."

Despite the similarities, though, these discontents got targeted quite differently.

In fact, Cape Kennedy and Akron seemed like parts of two different economies.

The worker resentments voiced in Akron reflected the traditional conflict of labor against big business. At Cape

Kennedy the space workers identified directly with the president-manager in Washington and his great spending machine.

Given the hardship that prevailed at the Cape, one would have expected a Democratic landslide. Actually, a rather heavy shift to Nixon was building up.

The driver for a linen company that supplied radiation coats at the Cape and linen service for local motels explained why. In 1968 when he voted for Hubert Humphrey his company had twelve routes. Early in 1972 it was down to only three routes.

He had been laid off for six months, which meant he could no longer meet house payments and had to go back to renting. Still he felt, "Nixon is for space and that will get us back to work."

This belief—or hope—that Nixon would support space and defense spending while the "Democrats are anti-space" was held quite generally.

Not long after the Florida primary, Cape Kennedy was chosen as one of the launching sites for the new space shuttle.

In both Akron and Cape Kennedy economic feelings molded attitudes toward the war. At the Cape, four of every five interviewed supported Nixon's Vietnam policies. Many shared the feelings of a Lockheed technician who was shifting to Nixon that "whenever there's a war there's money."

Another former Democrat swinging to Nixon, a twenty-nine-year-old data analyst for North American, complained, "I've been here seven years but could be laid off tomorrow."

He also felt, "There's no way of getting around needing war for our economy. Unless some new ecology program opens up or the space program opens, we'll have problems when the soldiers get back."

Asked about Vietnam, he said, "We have a commitment and shouldn't tuck our tails and run. Nixon has the right idea."

In Akron, though, opposition to the war was strong, with many workers arguing, "We don't need a war to keep people working," and "Let's pull out."

These war sentiments were particularly interesting since several Akron families had supported the war when interviewed in earlier years.

"I'm absolutely against pulling out," declared a Goodyear welder when interviewed in 1968. "We did the right thing in stepping in. Otherwise Communism would have spread. We can't leave those people alone over there; we'll have to step up the fighting."

The same welder, reinterviewed the day after the North Vietnamese offensive started, wanted to pull out. Now he complained, "I can't get overtime any more. We have men on layoff. When people retire they're not replaced."

Isolationist resentments streaked his talk. "We can't continue to take care of the whole world. Too much of our money is going worldwide."

This same targeting sequence—with economic adversity leading to opposition to Nixon and the war—was shown by a tire builder and his wife in nearby Barberton.

They had been for George Wallace in 1968 and for Robert Taft for Senate in 1970. At that time they favored Nixon's re-election, explaining, "He's not letting the colored get away with stuff. He stands behind policemen and we have policemen relatives."

In both 1970 and 1968, the wife repeated the same war feelings: "I don't believe in retreat. The United States shouldn't lower themselves to pulling out; we should win it."

By 1972, though, they were against Nixon and wanted to get out of Viet Nam. "We don't belong no place unless our country is threatened." the wife explained. "Why try to stop Communism if the people want it? Just stay in our own country and quit giving money away to foreigners; we need that money right here."

The husband, now sixty, added, "Firestone may put me on voluntary layoff and I'll get only 80 percent of my salary, or they may make me retire at sixty-two, which means a bad pension.

"I know the Democrats do too much for the colored," he went on, "but I think the Democrats can keep me working another five years."

His racial feelings, in short, had not changed, but he was ready to forget them to fight an economic grievance.

Another reinterview, with a thirty-seven-year-old Akron oiler, was intriguing in that over a four-year period he used the identical words to describe three different men whom he opposed.

During the 1968 presidential primaries, it was Robert Kennedy of whom the oiler said, "He's more for the colored people than anybody else. He's definitely out."

Shortly before the 1968 election—by then he was going for Wallace—it was, "Humphrey is more for the colored people than anybody else."

In 1972, this oiler was saying, "Nixon is more for colored people than anybody else. He babies them. I work with them and I know."

Obviously this oiler was not turning against Nixon for racial reasons. "I'll have to go Democrat," he explained. "Nixon is strictly for the rich, and I ain't rich. The rich man is trying to get rid of the unions; I have to go with the union because that's my bread and butter."

On the war, he thought, "Every country should take care of itself and not look to us. I would say pull out after being there that long." In 1968, he had wanted to step up the fighting.

The rubber companies were also being denounced for moving plants to the South or abroad. Despite this criticism of the companies, emotions got scrambled when the issue became one of taxing corporations in ways that might hurt their job-making ability.

In Barberton, Pittsburgh Plate and Glass was ordered to close part of its plant because of pollution. Three persons on the same street voiced conflicting views—each mirroring his or her own interest—on what should be done.

"My husband is a loader there. He'll be thrown out of work," argued one woman. "The government should help companies clean it up and keep people employed."

A rubber worker's wife thought, "The government should make these rich factories pay to stop the pollution. They've got the money. Tell 'em correct it or we'll shut you down."

The owner of the corner market seemed caught in between. "Pollution is a sorry subject here," he said. "It's cutting down our industry and hurting business.

"I don't know what to do. If the government helped PP&G, they'd have to help all companies and we'd all be broke. Frankly, I think PP&G has enough money to do it themselves, but they're too greedy."

3. Bombed-out Savings

One snowy morning in Pittsburgh a fifty-six-year-old man was pacing back and forth on the corner of Wolbridge and Herschel. "I'm waiting for the mailman," he explained. "I lost my job as diemaker when my company moved out. I'm supposed to start on this machinist job tonight. But it won't give me a pension. They'll make me retire at sixty-five. I'll be two months short of the ten years you need for pension.

"I took a civil-service exam for a government meat packer. If I get this letter saying I passed, then I won't go to this job tonight. It won't pay what I'd make as a diemaker, but this civil-service job will give me a pension.

"Otherwise," he concluded gloomily, "I'll have to work part-time jobs the rest of my life."

The desperate eagerness of this worker to obtain a job with a pension was only one illustration of how intense were the inflationary anxieties among many voters. The seven Vietnam war years had slashed by one-third the buying power of every dollar of savings, insurance, and pensions, as measured by the change in the cost-of-living index since 1965. With living costs still mounting from 3 to 4 percent a year, the prevailing expectation was that inflation would never end.

This dread of perpetual inflation and the continued uncertainty it casts over the future must be put down as one of the heavier costs of Vietnam.

For many persons, in fact, the traditional dream of retiring at sixty-five seemed to have collapsed like a bombed-out Vietnam shack. Some were fighting to stay on the job; others were searching out a second job; still others even wanted two pensions.

The twenty-three-year-old wife of a Maryland postal worker revealed that her husband planned to retire "as early as possible" —not to live out his years, but "so he'll have a pension and can get a second job, giving us two incomes."

In Tampa, a trouble man for the telephone company explained, "I'm forty-three, and I'll retire in seven years. I'll get a good pension from the telephone company after thirty years. But it won't be enough. I'll have to work after I retire."

A helpless shrug was the usual voter response to questions on how inflation can be stopped; nor was any decisive difference seen between Republicans and Democrats on that score.

Action by the government was not opposed on principle. On the contrary, the vast majority wanted controls on prices tightened. Even conservative Republicans volunteered that national health insurance would be needed for people to be able to pay soaring medical bills.

Few thought any populist scheme of redistributing taxes was a solution. The prime concern moving most people was how they could ease their own personal uncertainties over the future.

Defense and aerospace workers said, "We should have a government retirement plan so if a person works in different places he would still get a pension from all the places he worked."

A Curtiss-Wright worker in New Jersey recalled, "We had a great old guy at Wright's who was sixty-five years old and making only fifty cents an hour over what he would've gotten from his pension and social security. He was at Wright's for thirty-three years and all he wanted was to work, not for the money but just to keep busy, but they threw him out.

"We have six-dollar-an-hour machinists cleaning the lavatory for three dollars an hour just to hold on to their pensions."

A friend added, "Companies force you into early retirement that leaves you penniless when you get out."

Another outlet for these retirement fears was a kind of envy shopping—to try to obtain for one's own pension plan provisions that other workers might have.

City workers complained, "Policemen and firemen can get their pension after twenty years." Firemen grumbled, "Teachers have a better plan than the firefighters." Government workers compared their hospitalization benefits with those of factory workers.

With union members, overloading of bargaining demands served as a hedge against the future. Auto workers, for example, had fought for a pension system considered fairly generous in enabling a man to retire after thirty years' service at the age of fifty-eight in 1971 and fifty-six after 1972.

But a twenty-nine-year-old auto worker wanted the plan changed to be able to retire after thirty years regardless of age. "I've been there nine years," he explained, "so I could retire at fifty and get another job."

"My father", he added, "had thirty-five years with Ford. He gets $500 a month pension plus social security and he works part time."

Many other suggestions were advanced by individuals, virtually always for changes that would benefit them individually. Some of the exemptions urged were:

"When the man of the house retires, he shouldn't pay property taxes."

"Social security should be dropped to sixty years of age."

"The deduction for a dependent isn't enough."

As one looks back over those spring months of discontent, these thoughts stand out. The Democrats were unable to make any of the raging economic issues stick to Nixon's ribs.

Some of these splits in the economic solidarity of Democrats reflected lasting economic changes—the divisive effect of losing factories to the South or to foreign countries, the new orientation of defense and space workers to the president-manager in Washington, the hostility to welfare in dividing middle-class whites from the blacks.

It probably was shrewder politics to let people fight things out among themselves than to try to develop a common, unifying program.

By joining Wallace in attacking "government," Nixon did not do much more than direct many discontents away from himself. But that was about all he needed at the time.

North Vietnam's Easter offensive was soon to give Nixon an issue that was stronger than many economic grievances, and after that the job and overtime boom finally took hold.

Chapter 5

Vietnam—"with Honor"

1. "Like a Whipped Dog"

EASTER OF 1972 was still a day of political hope for the Democrats. Until North Vietnam's spring offensive began, my interviewing had shown no decisive breakthrough for Nixon.

While former Wallace supporters in the South were swinging heavily to the President, in the North they still talked of voting Democrat because of economic hardship that spring. Most first voters were lined up against the President. If the Democrats could hold their normal vote and pull heavily among young voters, Nixon could still be beaten.

Seven weeks later, though, Nixon was assured of re-election.

Hanoi's invasion was expected, of course, and one must assume that Nixon had taken every precaution for what was likely to happen. Still, one wonders whether a particular detail was planned for—the virtual rout of the South Vietnamese forces at the start of the fighting. Without those early reverses Nixon may not have gained the complete psychological triumph that was to come.

Through all of April and into mid-May the headlines shrieked possible defeat or collapse of the South Vietnamese armies—"Quang Tri Falls to Foe". . ."Saigon Threatened" . . ."Kontum Besieged". . ."Hue Gripped by Panic as Enemy Drives On". . ."Reds Rip Base near Pleiku."

To many Americans it was not South Vietnam but the United States that was being defeated. Often they exploded in profanity, with remarks like "Don't crawl out on our bellies" or "We can't run like a whipped dog."

Some wanted to send American troops back in, to "invade North Vietnam and win," others to "just show them what we can do."

A Denver housewife urged, "Ask for volunteers to go over and invade North Vietnam. Level the place and then pull out."

High praise of Harry Truman began to pepper my notes. What people liked about Truman, it turned out, was that "he had the courage to drop the big bomb on those Orientals."

A fifty-year-old attorney who worked for the Maryland state government argued vehemently, "We should send American troops back there and really give it to them. We ought to drop a nuclear bomb on them."

"What makes it so important for us to win in Vietnam?" I asked.

He paused, shrugged his shoulders, and replied, "I don't think Vietnam is important to us at all. It's a matter of pride. This country has never been whipped. I'm like the Chinese. I just want to save face."

Others who talked of using nuclear weapons turned out to be bluffing. A GM assembly worker near Baltimore felt, "If we show them we mean business, they'll stop. Use the nuclear threat like we did before. It worked with the Korean war."

"Would you actually use the nuclear bombs?"

"No, I'd just threaten them."

"Why, then, should they believe us?"

He hesitated, then replied, "Nuclear weapons are terrible things."

Other Americans—particularly those with sons of draft age—were ready to write off South Vietnam. A Pittsburgh policeman declared, "We should quit now, just say everybody out, we quit. I'm a law-and-order man, but I'll go to jail with my four sons before they're sent to Vietnam."

Four years earlier, when first interviewed, he had been sharply critical of a cousin who had gone to Canada.

"I called that kid every name in the book," the policeman recalled, "but at least he's alive. I'd like to hear someone say, 'Let's put this country back on its feet and take care of our own doorstep.'"

Often during those anxious weeks husbands and wives while being interviewed would break into angry arguments. Usually the husband would be urging stronger military action, while the wife wanted out.

In one Maryland suburb a burglar-alarm installer declared, "Make an all-out invasion. Why give up after all these years? It's time to win."

His wife interrupted scornfully, "You call yourself a military man; well, I'm just a mother. This government will never get my sons. I don't go for our bombing. I carried my two boys nine months inside my body. I'm not sending them over for a lost cause in a country that ain't worth a pot of dirt."

On Monday, May 8, came the dropping of aerial mines in Haiphong Harbor and the blockade of Hanoi's waters. That action, my interviews showed, started the big swing to Nixon of voters who had backed Hubert Humphrey or George Wallace in 1968.

"He stood up to Russia, and that took guts" was a widespread reaction. The rankling sense of humiliation over threatened defeat was replaced by a sense of vindication. Many voters had been contending for years that "the only way to fight it is go in to win or get out."

Not only did Nixon clinch re-election in those weeks but at that point in time, as I later wrote, he also gained a free hand to resist congressional and public pressures for withdrawal from Vietnam before the election.

Congress still had before it a resolution calling for withdrawal by some fixed date. Even had it been passed, Nixon had the voter support to ignore it.

"Bomb them into giving up" was the usual reply given by voters to the question, "What should be done now in Vietnam?" Generally the voters interviewed thought "we should stay in Vietnam as long as is needed for a settlement 'with honor' "—or, as many put it openly, that would "save face."

Expectations of being out of Vietnam by election time were chalked off.

In a Maryland suburb the wife of an FBI agent protested, "The way it is now, I'd send my son to Canada."

Her husband talked her down by arguing, "We're starting to hurt them now. I wouldn't let up. Traitors like Jane Fonda should be shot."

The dominant mood, in short, shifted to being one of "Show them who's boss" and "Don't let up when we have them on the run" and "Bring them to their knees."

The more impassioned attacks on Senator George McGovern reflected rage that "he wants to back down when we have them scared" or "he'd pull out just when we're winning."

Often these angers overrode strong economic grievances. A Penn Central freight conductor in the Buffalo suburb of

Cheektowaga began our interview with a bitter tirade against Nixon as "just a tool of business."

He raged on, "They're talking of shutting down part of the railroad. No one has anything to ship. Carloadings are going down. They're laying us off."

Asked who he wanted to see elected president, he retorted, "I can't vote for McGovern. He'd surrender the country."

A fireman in Rock Island, Illinois, protested, "Nixon is letting big business run rampant. I'm poorer because price control isn't working. Taxes are inequitable and going up and nothing's been done about it."

Still, when asked about McGovern, he said, "I don't like McGovern's appeasement of the North Vietnamese. I'd like to see us out, but with honor. I like to save face."

2. The McGovern Rocket

George McGovern's White House chances had also been riding on Hanoi's offensive. At first, the stepped-up fighting in Vietnam brought McGovern a significant boost in voter support, which helped his candidacy through the final primaries and the nomination, even though his appeal had begun to slide before the Miami convention opened.

One interview was particularly revealing in this regard. On the weekend before Nixon mined Haiphong Harbor, I was doing my interviewing in an east Baltimore suburb where George Wallace drew 31 percent of the vote in 1968.

At one house a forty-eight-year-old plasterer declared, "We haven't been fighting this war the right way. We shouldn't just slap them on the wrist. Go in and blockade them. They can't fight without food and weapons."

His wife, who had come out to join our conversation, disagreed sharply with her husband. "I'm afraid it's too late for that. Let's get out. Our only son is in the Navy until 1973. Betty down the street has a boy on a ship waiting off Saigon. He writes her terrible letters. The woman next door has a son in the Marines.

"We've done all we can for the South Vietnamese," she went on. "They can't fight without us and we can't do their fighting for them."

Both she and her husband had voted for Wallace in 1968. "I may vote for McGovern this time," she volunteered. "They say he's a hard-nosed radical, but I don't believe it. He's the peace candidate."

When I revisited this couple after Nixon's return from Moscow, both were voting for Nixon. On McGovern, the wife now thought, "He's all right, but he changes his mind too much."

That shift in her feeling is characteristic voter psychology. When voters see a man serving their political needs, as did this wife concerning the war when we first talked, they will defend the candidate from all attacks. When they no longer need the candidate they see all his weaknesses.

This woman's reaction wasn't unusual.

Any number of other voters had fixed their hopes for peace on McGovern, at least briefly, as insurance against the failure of Nixon's actions. What if the waves of B-52s that Nixon ordered out did not halt Hanoi's offensive and the miserable war was lengthened? If that happened, these voters wanted a Democrat to turn to who would be sure to pull us out of Vietnam.

The Easter offensive, in other words, did not spur the voters to prefer a "center" candidate for the Democratic nomination, at least as far as the war was concerned.

In the end the voters might turn against him as an "extremist" or even as a "coward," but as long as the outcome of

Hanoi's offensive was in doubt, there was support for a Democrat whose views on the war would be as different from Nixon's as possible.

Whether Nixon anticipated such a voter reaction makes intriguing speculation. Still, it is worth noting by those who think the "middle ground" is the only political ground to stand on. Every conflict generates its own dynamics.

One evidence of the strength of this reaction was a burst of McGovern support among Republican voters in early May. At the time, I was interviewing extensively on Maryland's presidential primary and also supervising a *Washington Star* survey in the state. Both my own interviewing and the *Star* survey caught a shift of youngish Republicans who had voted for Nixon in 1968 but who were ready to vote for McGovern in November. These shifters would take no other Democratic candidate—neither Humphrey nor Muskie. The war was the issue that troubled them, and on that issue they were prepared to break party lines for a "peace candidate."

On the day of the Maryland primary, one mother, whose husband owned a window-cleaning business, explained why she had voted for McGovern that morning, although she had been for Nixon in 1968.

"I know the Communists are trying to take over the world," she said, "but I can't see sending any more of our boys over there to be killed. My son is eleven, and I'm hoping so much for peace.

"If the mining and bombing will help bring our troops home faster," she continued, "then good for Nixon. But if the war gets any worse, maybe we should give McGovern a try.

"I'll wait and see what happens," she went on. "I don't think McGovern would pull out all at once. He wouldn't desert our POWs."

In Laurel, Maryland, three young couples, who were interviewed as they left the polls, said that as registered Republicans they hadn't voted in the Democratic primary but favored McGovern in November.

Some of these Republicans actually voted for McGovern in November.

A civil servant in Laurel, always Republican in the past, explained when interviewed in May, "I agree with bombing to protect the Americans left there, but I couldn't care less what happens to the South Vietnamese.

"I'm a conservative, but McGovern I still like," he added.

Reinterviewed in October, he was upset about "pressure groups buying their way into government. First it was ITT, then the Dairy Association scandal, then the Watergate. Day after day, you hear favoritism and more favoritism. The only way to get rid of it is to throw the administration out. I think McGovern is as honest a person as he can be."

But these converts proved not too numerous and were more than offset by the shift against McGovern among Democratic families.

Haiphong sparked a turn against McGovern among first voters as well. A steelworker's son, red-bearded, recalled, "When Nixon dropped those mines, I thought to myself it means a bigger war. They're going to come and get me.

"But," the youth added, "the Russians didn't do anything. Nixon's plan worked."

This swift swing in voter sentiment largely explains why the door-to-door canvassing for McGovern, which had been so successful during the primaries, failed for the general election. During the presidential primaries, the McGovern youths had a cause that could be expressed quite simply: "McGovern is the peace candidate" or "McGovern will end the war." But when these canvassers rang doorbells in the later months of the campaign the message was no longer that simple. The prevailing sentiment was that Nixon had the war in hand and would end it in time.

Also, the McGovernites weren't alone in ringing doorbells and reaching individual voters. A parts clerk, only nineteen, had voted McGovern in the Maryland primary. "My lottery number was 66," he recalled, "and I felt sure I'd be taken. Then in June I got this telephone call from a recruiting sergeant. He was calling all the low lottery number fellows in the area. He explained how I could get out of the draft by signing up for six months in the National Guard. I'm for Nixon now. He kept his promise to get us out of the war."

Through the whole summer there remained many families who still feared that continued bombings would not make peace.

"My husband calls me a quitter," said one mother in Rock Island, Illinois, "but I don't see why we can't bring everybody home. I have three boys, and with what Women's Lib is saying about equal rights, my girls will have to go, too."

In West York, Pennsylvania, a grinder's wife, always Republican before, said, "I'm becoming more and more concerned about the war. Our oldest son is seventeen, and we have four more coming up. The South Vietnamese are relying on us too much and not trying hard enough on their own. McGovern's war stand is his one good issue."

A fireman's wife in Rochester started the interview by saying, "We must stick with the President on the war. But I don't think we can bomb those people into submission. I have a brother who is sixteen. How long will the war go on?

"My parents are Republicans," she continued. "Mother argues with father, 'Dump Nixon and get this war ended.' But when I tell this to my husband, he says if we pull out now the unemployment would be terrible."

While we were at war, enormous economic changes took

place. American investment abroad in multinational corporations nearly doubled, one effect being to spread technological
advances and to integrate the economies of nations.

During these same years, we shifted from a trade surplus
to a trade deficit. Before we got into war in 1965, the U.S. trade
balance was averaging an export surplus of $5.4 billion a year.
By 1971, it had shifted to a deficit of $2.7 billion, and in 1972,
to a $6.8 billion deficit, even after one dollar devaluation.

Inside this country a sharply changed structure of economic interest has been built. New fortunes, some of them in
paper assets, have been created; old savings have been enlarged
for some, greatly reduced in real value for many families.

For the future we are left with the task of regaining our
balance and stability as a people, even while the United States
as a whole must find a new balance in relation to the rest of
the world. At the year's end the unemployment rate remained
at 5 percent; devaluation would be expected to increase the
inflation.

From Vietnam "with honor"; from home and abroad:
what will these two phrases come to mean? Some feeling for
what lies ahead may come from looking at the effects of
sharpening economic and social competition here at home.
What is being squeezed out? What is being strengthened?

Chapter 6

Welfare and
the Work Ethic

1. "Live It Up . . ."

NOT MUCH INTERVIEWING was needed to discover that "welfare" had become the 1972 carrier of racial backlash resentments in people's minds, much as "law and order" was in 1968.

Voters who urged, "Get them off welfare," would almost always go on to talk of blacks. Usually the key thought in their protest would be, "The government keeps giving them things," while "whites have to work for what they get."

When welfare was brought up in connection with white people, it generally was praised.

Near Richmond, Virginia, a traffic signalman said, "People knock welfare, but when my father got sick I saw how some people really need it."

A retired Air Force pilot had separated from his wife and

they were getting a divorce. There were three children. He felt, "Welfare is a good thing for divorced women. So damn many women never get through high school. They should be given an income so they don't have to shack up with some guy."

But perhaps the most revealing feature of the welfare agitation, which intensified as the campaign wore on, was what it disclosed about the dynamics of competitive individualism and the "work ethic."

One argument advanced on behalf of individualism is that it enables people who work hard to keep more of their own earnings. A black recreation director in the city of Washington demanded, "Welfare should be cut out. I got five kids to take care of. Taxes are high enough without welfare. Make the women who have these kids tell who the fathers are so they'll support them.

"If my daughter got pregnant," he went on, "I'd make her work to support that kid if she didn't tell who the father was. I took a job for $48 a week and I made it, but somebody else would rather take a handout."

But the same language could be employed to avoid paying one's fair share of taxes or to cut loose from and ignore the whole welfare problem as unmanageable.

The mining of Hanoi's harbors and the stepped-up bombing jumped the costs of the war. Also, on his return from Moscow, early in June, Nixon announced that the SALT agreement would increase, not reduce, arms spending. These greater military commitments, along with continued inflation, dashed hopes of any tax reduction. Instead, the prospect being headlined was for higher taxes after the election.

One could picture the public's tax-cutting emotions being forced into a narrow pass, with insurmountable hills on each side, which brought them out with one visible target against which to expend their wrath—the costs of welfare.

We had been asking voters what kind of government spending they would cut. What would they increase?

Before the North Vietnam offensive, responses favored reductions in space, military, and defense spending. As the war escalated, pressures to lower defense spending were shelved and anti-welfare feeling surged. For some families it built up into an issue whose emotional agitation even overshadowed concern over the war.

"We talk about welfare every night," remarked an elderly Rochester contractor. "It upsets us so much."

"I tell my children to live it up while you can," interjected his wife. "I tell them don't bother working and saving like we did. Just spend all your money and then go on welfare.

"I was born in Italy," she recalled. "When I came here as a girl, I was called a wop and a dago. Companies wouldn't hire an Italian or a Catholic. Now the government makes them hire colored.

"Our taxes have gone up 500 percent," she continued. "The colored are getting food stamps and I have to pay for it."

Her husband protested, "The tax system leaves these big shots free and we pay it all."

The same two welfare jokes cropped up across the country. "I was standing in line at the supermarket," one tale ran. "I saw this guy with two carts full of groceries. The bill was $200 and he paid for it all with food stamps. Oh, brother! I followed him out to the parking lot, and what kind of car do you think he had? A brand-new Cadillac convertible!"

The second welfare story was often repeated when a husband and wife were interviewed together. The dialogue was almost like a TV skit. The husband or wife would begin by protesting, "We can't deduct as much for dependents as they get to raise their kids on welfare." The interchange that followed ran something like this:

The husband: "I'm gonna quit my job and let welfare make my house payments."

His wife: "I'll fix you a bedroom in the basement, honey. Then they'll give me ADC."

Other wives would quip, "I told my husband, leave me and we'll get a government check."

Meanwhile McGovern had been gaining attention as the likely Democratic nominee. Quick publicity was being turned onto a proposal he had made in January, but which drew no notice then, that each person be given $1,000 as part of a negative income tax scheme.

"He wants to take our money and give it to the colored who won't work" was a common voter reaction. Until then, with Humphrey drawing the bulk of the black vote, McGovern had not been thought of as particularly pro-Negro.

McGovern's arguments for cutting defense spending were rejected with a curt "He wants to cut defense so he can blow the money on welfare."

Other voters cracked, "Where's he going to get all those thousand-dollar bills?"

By early August I was writing that Nixon's own Family Assistance Plan, then still pending in Congress, would meet with just as hostile a public reaction as McGovern's plan had.

Nixon's Family Assistance Plan was ditched.

2. More Socialism Wanted?

In a Labor Day talk the President decided to capitalize on McGovern's troubles by picturing the election as a choice between the "work ethic" and the "welfare ethic"—a theme which he was to return to after the election.

Actually, on no issue were the two candidates closer in their expressed views. It had been Nixon, in fact, who first proposed that the "working poor"—families whose earnings fell below the poverty line—be given cash supplements. This innovation was part of the Family Assistance Plan that Nixon sent to Congress in August 1969.

Praised highly by liberals, the original proposal called for a basic annual income floor of $1,600 for a family of four. An estimated 1.2 million persons would have been added to the welfare rolls, which would have cost the federal government an additional $3.8 billion a year at the outset. Most of the new welfare recipients would have been white, largely from the South; yet Southerners in Congress opposed the legislation.

Calling for "an end to hunger in America for all time," the President in 1969 also nearly doubled the food-stamp appropriation.

By 1971 the number of food-stamp participants had more than tripled—from 3.2 million in 1969 to 10.5 million.

Back in 1969 the President apparently thought that black voters might be added to his "new Republican majority." In 1969 he also reduced taxes, which cut available funds for public programs. In 1971, he proposed postponing his welfare program even while he was giving to business, as Charles Schultze of Brookings pointed out, "$8 billion in additional tax relief." By 1972, welfare was politically expendable.

As for the voters themselves, many of the complaints about welfare reflected feelings of envy by taxpayers who would have liked the same benefits from the government.

A heavy-equipment operator in York, Pennsylvania, echoed a common feeling when he protested, "People on welfare have it better than people who work. They don't pay taxes, but they get free medical and dental care, free eyeglasses, plus two checks a month."

Attacks on food stamps often traced back to inflation-kindled angers that "people on welfare eat Delmonico steaks while we have to eat hamburger."

This same competitive sense explained the protest of a retired pharmacist in San Bruno, California: "McGovern wants to give them too much. People who work all their lives, all they get is social security. These people who won't work will get more."

We misjudge the public temper if such reactions are regarded as evidence of an anti-government philosophy. The voters were not opposing the use of government on their own behalf; they were objecting to welfare recipients' getting benefits free that taxpayers had to pay for.

"The rich don't pay a dime in taxes and the poor don't pay a cent" was another common gripe.

Often, though, higher earnings did not make for a greater sense of public responsibility.

"As far as I'm concerned, these taxes are pure stealing," protested a Michigan truck driver. "I work fifteen hours a day and make $400 a week, but I pay $100 a week in taxes. It makes me sick when they take my taxes to give it to second and third generations living off welfare."

Still, he urged an increase in defense spending and labeled McGovern a "yellow-streaked, gutless coward" for wanting to pull out of Vietnam.

A machinist in Lancaster, Pennsylvania, who was shifting to Nixon from Humphrey in 1968, also thought, "McGovern would just hand it over to the Communists. It's like admitting defeat.

"We can't afford to cut defense," he maintained. "We've got to stay strong."

Where did he stand on taxes?

"They just pass these taxes and there's no chance to object. I say hand government back to the people. Working men all over this country are paying to run it, but we have no say."

He wanted social security dropped to sixty years of age and a more liberal pension from his company, including "a thirty-year plan in the factories just like the steelworkers and government workers get."

This machinist was expecting striking improvements in his living. Still, on welfare he felt, "One of our biggest problems in this country is too much free money being handed out."

3. The Cost-Plus Ethic

At first the comment of this Curtiss-Wright welder in New Jersey seemed no different from other welfare remarks we had been picking up.

He had talked of "girls I know gettin' welfare who make $3,000 a year on the side as go-go dancers. Those people live better than I do."

Then he began talking about the cost-plus contract for submarine reactors that his company had been awarded.

"These contracts are great!" he said. "I work only two and a half days a week, including Saturday and Sunday, and still get paid the same as if I worked five weekdays. I was going in only two or three days a week last year, and still made over $11,000."

As he talked, it became clear that the "cost-plus ethic" nourished abuses on an astonishing scale.

I began collecting tales of cost-plus as they came from random interviewing. The numbers of the stories related suggested that the practice was taken for granted.

In Huntington Park, California, a twenty-five-year-old electronics technician for Hughes Aircraft had a "high" on cost-plus, saying, "The company gets real free with overtime. We get more, so we spend more. It's great for the economy."

His parents, whom I had interviewed in two earlier elections, were staunch Democrats from Minnesota. The son had

gone for Humphrey in 1968—"he was always big on aerospace"—but was now strong for Nixon.

"Nixon is shooting for full employment," he explained.
"Three years ago things weren't too good, but now North
American's got that new contract and Hughes is doing real
well. Things are really looking up."

Other aerospace workers whose companies had not gotten
new contracts weren't so happy over cost-plus.

An engraver at McDonnell Douglas grumbled over the
"higher taxes everybody has to pay" as she recalled the old
cost-plus days when the bite was on the other fellow:

"They used to tell us we had to work on Saturdays. When
we went in it was just a playday with nothing to do. We'd get
time and a half for Saturday, and then they'd tell us to stay
home on Monday. We were on cost-plus, and they had to
spend the money, I guess.

"We used to have to fill out these time cards for every job.
There were jobs I could do in fifteen minutes, but they'd make
me put down four hours for it. We had it that way for three
years, and then things started slowing down and the layoffs
started."

The wife of a forty-nine-year-old Northrop Aircraft in-
spector complained, "Work is still up and down; it's not what
it used to be. I don't like cost-plus contracts at all. These
companies take advantage and throw the money away because
it's not theirs. Everybody gets fat off them, and when the
contract is up you're poor again."

In Long Beach a father and son were both working with
cost-plus companies. The father, who was with Hughes, recalled, "I registered Democrat when I was twenty-one years
old, and I changed my registration two weeks ago to Republican. The Democrats have gotten away from what they used to
be in the Roosevelt days.

"They're getting too socialistic," he went on, "getting into too much of what belongs to the people. They're taking on too much of business. Now I got this rental unit here, and the government can't tell me who can live in it.

"Taxes are too high," the father added. "Let's have a state lottery and lower my property taxes."

The son, who was an accounts representative for Southern California Edison, felt, "It's too easy to get on welfare and have a million kids."

He thought, "Cost-plus is fine, real good. When they put in a new freeway, we make a lot of money moving our lines."

In 1968, the son recalled, "I voted for Nixon, and I was a registered Democrat at the time. But I changed my registration to Republican two years ago when I voted for Governor Reagan. I'm big on free enterprise. It's not a sin to go out and make a profit like McGovern thinks; the Democrats are too much for socialism."

Both this son and his father had changed their party registration because "the Democrats are too socialistic." But what was the difference between "socialism" and "cost-plus"? Under cost-plus both apparently got more from the government—that is, from other taxpayers—than they might have gotten under normal business practices.

In one of his speeches President Nixon pictured the nation facing a choice between a work ethic based on self-reliance and a welfare ethic based on government.

Certainly that "choice" doesn't describe what is happening in the country. Like any system of organizing rewards and responsibilities, competitive individualism has its strengths and faults.

Some workers, satisfied that they themselves are employed, shrug off unemployment by saying, "There are plenty of jobs around if people want to work."

Others urge that more work be created. The wife of a furnace tender in Kenosha, Wisconsin, a Democrat sticking with McGovern, protested, "Our son couldn't get a scholarship for medical school because we're not poor enough. If we were on relief, our son could get all the aid he wanted.

"Years ago we had WPA," she added. "Why can't the government put people to work?"

Still others would use the "work ethic" as a kind of neighborhood selector through which blacks who don't "shape up" can be excluded.

A heat-treat operator's wife argued, "I'm for open housing. If they can pay for the house, they won't be on welfare."

A truck driver urged, "Let the housing determine the integration. That'd be the natural way to integrate. I wouldn't have any objection to a colored person living next door, cause then he'd be paying the same taxes I do."

There is also some feeling that only taxpayers should have an effective voice in politics. A retired auto worker conceded, "Nixon is all for the money people, but McGovern is for hippies, yippies, and colored people. I have nothing against them, but they're not paying the bills."

"Make them work" also struck many families as an effective way of correcting welfare abuses.

"It's a racket; they collect eight different checks under eight different names," protested a New York salesman.

In Farmingdale, New York, the eighteen-year-old son of a butcher told how "people come into my father's store and buy meat for their dogs with food stamps. They ask for liver for their dog. That gets my father mad. That's our tax money being used to feed dogs!"

Chapter 7

Will Defense
Divide Us?

1. Wanted: A Growth Industry

THE 1972 CAMPAIGN posed one truly agonizing political question—can a military-industrial job complex that spends $80 billion a year and provides 6 million jobs be voted out of offiice?

To that, the President's 1974 budget message added another disturber—will the defense establishment be managed politically so that it divides the country it is supposed to protect?

The city of Fredericksburg, Virginia, halfway between the Pentagon and Richmond, provides a sensitive setting for exploring both questions. No military or space hardware is manufactured in the city. Still, its main source of employment by far comes from nearby military installations—Fort Belvoir and the

Pentagon, the Quantico Marine barracks, the Naval Proving Grounds at Dahlgren, the A. P. Hill tank-testing center.

Moreover, these defense jobs offer better pay and more opportunity for advancement than any non-military employers in the area.

The Food Machine Corporation operates one of the largest cellophane plants in the world, but three FMC workers I came across in my interviewing spoke bitterly about the company's labor relations.

For women, three or four clothing factories offer work at piecework rates. An unskilled high-school graduate can start as a clerk at $80 a week in town; at a military post the beginning pay runs $5,100 a year.

Often, working for defense becomes a family affair. On Beauregard Street a twenty-three-year-old woman said, "My father and uncle are mechanics at Fort Belvoir. When I finished high school, my father helped me get work there as a secretary. My husband is on the Belvoir waiting list."

A department manager at Montgomery Ward, he had applied to Fort Belvoir in the summer of 1971. His wife recalled, "It would have meant taking a cut in pay right away, but working for the government is better in the long run."

He had passed all requirements and was ready to start work when Nixon announced a ceiling on new hirings in the federal government.

That job freeze and other economy moves angered not only her husband but, as our interviewing at the time showed, workers in the area generally.

A heavy-duty foreman at Quantico, whose wife was a budget clerk there, protested, "Money is so tight at the base we have a standing order that if someone retires we can't replace him. We're three mechanics short in my shop alone."

A Wallace supporter in 1968, he explained, "I'm hoping

to vote Democrat next time. Nixon is all for big corporations, and he doesn't care about labor. Big business is making excess profits at the expense of the working man."

A power-plant laborer complained, "We've had layoffs, and more are coming up. I'm low man on the ladder in our department."

For Nixon in 1968, he felt, "we can't stand another Republican president until we get more jobs. He's trying to curb inflation, but he's threatening my job. The man is trying, but it's getting to me."

By the summer of 1972, though, the mood around Fredericksburg had changed. A utilities worker explained, "It's a hell of a thing to say, but our economy needs a war. Defense spending should be increased to make more jobs for people."

In the previous summer, after having been laid off for seven months, this utilities worker was an angry presidential critic. He wanted to "cut defense and all foreign aid" to "spend more money over here."

At least two points stand out from this Fredericksburg sketch:

(1) For many areas, defense is the only growth industry, with few other work outlets.

(2) Defense workers can be quick on the political draw in resisting any employment threat.

When Nixon ordered a ceiling on new hiring during the summer of 1971, many Fredericksburg workers turned against him; when McGovern became the threat, they swung against him.

In itself, there is nothing surprising or sinister about such voting behavior. Americans have always used the ballot to advance their own economic interests, whether it has been as farmers, workers, businessmen, ditchdiggers, or as members of any other occupation.

In the context of a total politics, anything that exists becomes a political force for its own continuance and even expansion.

The military-industrial job complex, though, generates both political stability and instability. It represents a sizable voting constituency, directly responsive to the president's manipulations, which can generally be counted on to support the government's foreign and defense policies.

On the menacing side, cost-plus abuses and overruns of military spending threaten constantly to become unmanageable. Also, Defense's one-third share of the total federal budget clashes with virtually every demand for civilian spending and could, in fact, frustrate all hopes for any change in economic priorities.

Instead of trying to reconcile this built-in conflict, Nixon's actions seem to be turning it into a major political divider in the nation. Defense increases are lined up in his 1974 budget much like a firing squad taking aim at social programs that are to be shot down.

The President must have expected that the Democrats, not the Marines, would rush to the rescue of these condemned social programs and even demand cuts in defense spending— which could enable him to tag the Democrats as anti-defense and "isolationist."

My own bias on this corresponds pretty much with the views of Bernard M. Baruch, with whom I worked during World War II. We should spend whatever is needed for defense and for an effective deterrent against nuclear attack. These weapons should be paid for in higher taxes. The cost can certainly be met by a nation with a median family income running over $10,000 a year.

If taxes are not to be raised and military wastes are not cut, the firing-squad drama of defense against social programs could be re-enacted annually. Defense expenditures will be climbing quite heavily in the future. Despite the SALT agreements, the Navy has to speed its strategic efforts to counter Soviet submarine development. Eventually, billions will go into the new Trident system of long-range underwater submarines with accompanying missiles, to replace Poseidon subs as nuclear deterrents that cannot be knocked out by a Soviet first strike.

While future defense budgets swell, Nixon—unless popular resistance changes his strategy—may be ordering further reductions in social programs or try to block any social increases that the Democrats might push.

By failing to balance defense and social needs, Nixon risks undercutting sustained public support for a sound defense and foreign policy.

His decision to cast defense and social programs in antagonistic roles, as hero and villain, may be an encore performance of how he handled McGovern's assault on defense spending.

What Nixon did was clever but not a great political feat. He simply timed his political fire so that defense spending would increase—with three to four billions more in new contracts going out—just when McGovern was pressing for defense reductions.

McGovern was put in the position of resurrecting fears of new defense unemployment, while Nixon appeared as the protector of defense jobs.

A fifty-year-old mechanic at the Naval Ordnance Station in Indianhead, Maryland, talked proudly of how "I worked on those guns that are sitting on our ship forty-two miles from Hanoi.

"I had no use for Nixon when they were going to close our plant down a year ago. We lost a hundred people who weren't replaced.

"Now it looks like they'll keep us open," he continued. "We got five new contracts to build guns for Vietnam, and they're hiring 800 more men."

Again, a forty-one-year-old Navy pipe fitter in South Philadelphia recalled, "When Nixon started these defense cutbacks a couple years ago, I never thought I'd have to vote for him. But McGovern would be worse.

"We've had quite a few layoffs. We had twenty men in the shop. Now only nine do the same work.

"It seems like we need a war in our economy," he went on. "But there's lots of work in the cities and states that could be done."

Other defense workers had gone through the earlier Nixon years fearful that they might be forced into retirement or be let out under "Reduction in Force" (RIF) orders.

At York, Pennsylvania, a purchasing agent for the Naval Ships Parts Control Center talked of voting Republican "for the first time in my life."

He explained, "McGovern will knock out the defense picture and that means jobs. We've had our layoffs, and they're about over with now. McGovern would start them up again."

It turned out he had been under pressure to take early retirement. "They tried to get people to retire a little earlier. Some men did, and then they couldn't get anything else.

"But I couldn't retire now, not with a daughter in high school. If she decides to go to college, I couldn't retire until she graduated."

A similar reaction was voiced by a Navy wife in Fredericksburg, who was also shifting to Nixon. She worked as a secretary at Fort Belvoir while her husband did research on ocean currents for the Navy.

"There have been several RIFs in the past year," she recalled, "and we still have our fingers crossed. I don't trust McGovern. He says he'll pull out of Vietnam in thirty days.

I don't think he can do it. His tax proposals will cut out our jobs.

"A lot of people will be out of work if we pull out of Vietnam," she went on. "We don't need a war, but we should spend more money at home building ships and planes for our own defense."

2. Home Fires Burning

"Let's build the SST, and when it's finished scrap it. We need these throwaway programs to keep people employed."

The sheet-metal mechanic in Long Beach, California, who made this suggestion was deadly serious. He had just finished working on the construction of a peanut-butter factory, but recalled, "Things were so slow I was out of work six months last year. I think the boom is over."

Since $5.5 billion was the estimated starting-up cost of the SST, this mechanic's suggestion might seem extreme. Still, many Americans across the country share his feeling that some part of defense spending has become a modernized version of the WPA that Franklin Roosevelt organized during the Depression.

These misgivings about defense spending add additional strains to the President's psychological gamble of building "peace" upon higher military spending while important domestic needs are neglected.

Toward the end of the campaign, particularly after Henry Kissinger's "peace is at hand" statement, many more persons began urging that defense spending should be cut, often adding "up to a point" or "not as much as McGovern wants."

There were also repeated urgings to "take that money being spent in Vietnam and put it into this country."

These comments reflect the generally held feeling that the war years have left distortions and neglects here at home that need correcting. Ordinarily, one would expect a president to turn inward with the American people.

Up to now, though, Nixon's priority decisions have not been directed toward restoring a balanced American society. He has seemed more concerned with establishing a power structure which would give top priority to defense and economic expansion abroad, leaving other needs to forage for themselves.

An unbalanced economy transmits uneasy messages. Defense workers reveal their own uneasiness when they say, "We don't have to be at war as long as we keep up defense spending," or "We can always make weapons and just store them up."

Other voters are troubled because of so little real conversion to peacetime industry. A month before the election a machinist's wife in York, a Republican sticking with Nixon, talked of how her husband had just begun working overtime on a new defense contract. The company made chains for ships.

She went on to say, "We could use that Vietnam money here to build houses and roads and parks and schools. The factory where my husband works, I've often wondered why they couldn't make chains for swings in the park."

High defense spending coupled with high unemployment also keeps alive fears of another war, particularly among families with young sons. All through the war, the troubling question stirred in the minds of voters, "Do we need a war to prosper?"

The President's talk of "prosperity without war" or "a generation of peace" had little effect.

A utilities worker, in his thirties, was strong for Nixon, defending everything the President had done. Still, when asked about Nixon's promise of "a generation of peace," this utilities worker, shaking his head in disbelief, said, "Our economy needs a war. It's the one thing that starts a lot of investment going. They'll decide when we should have another war."

Coalitions can be built in varied ways. Nixon seems to be constructing his on the basis of the enemies he picks. Our defense budget could have been handled as an expense to be shared by the whole citizenry, with business and the well-to-do paying their share.

Instead Nixon has joined together "the taxpayer," defense spending, and foreign economic expansion against social programs at home—a rather uneven political contest one must concede.

The structured quality of this cleavage suggests that it would be well to examine in greater detail what kind of political coalition Nixon has been assembling.

To gain social and economic stability, must we follow the course of dividing the country? Or is there an alternative of common goals and unifying purposes?

Chapter 8

The Shape-up
Coalition

1. The Entry Generation

BY MIDSUMMER it seemed that "the shape-up coalition" might be the appropriate label for the new majority that Nixon was attracting.

That term was suggested by interviews with two first voters in the borough of Queens in New York City. One, a McGovern supporter and a twenty-one-year-old senior in computer engineering, refused to "shape up" and fit the economy as it stood; the other, a pro-Nixon voter, felt set for life economically, having been admitted to the electricians' union.

The pro-Nixon youth, who was twenty, had started college but dropped out "to go into the trades." His mother talked proudly of how "4,000 persons applied to become apprentice electricians but only 700 were accepted." After five years as an apprentice, she added, "He'll make ten dollars an hour."

The McGovernite had worked as a gas-station attendant over the summer, and intended to major in conservation engineering at Brooklyn Polytech. "Nixon is for defense buildup and the war machine," he felt. "McGovern is for research in ecology."

As a likely computer analyst, he faced a curious job choice. "You can work for IBM," he said, "but then you must wear a 'sincere' tie and cut your hair. I won't do that. I'll be doing digital work, like in a bank.

"You should see these digital guys in the back of a bank," he added, "with their beards and their hair down their backs."

That clash in the work choices of these two youths mirrors the "ins" versus "outs" division that was the pattern of both Nixon's victory and of his second term.

Not yet structured into the party system—it may dominate both parties—this "shape-up" psychology is becoming the stamp of economic and political power in the nation.

Suburbs, with their growing proportion of available jobs, are being looked on as the white man's turf—"only the colored who pay taxes can move in here."

Under revenue sharing as Nixon wants it, all claimants— from clinics for the retarded to property tax protestors—are being forced to justify their existence before state and local officials, knowing that funds are not available even if all were ready to shape up.

A Washington-area bank requires a married couple to consent to birth control as a condition for a loan.

The system of rewards and penalties, barriers and openings, that is being developed has two key characteristics—it limits access into the privileged, walled sectors and seeks to throw the burdens of economic and social dislocations onto those outside the walls.

For this chapter, my examination of this coalition of walls is organized largely in terms of young voters. First, as they seek economic entry, another four million each year, they will be testing every door in the economy. Second, they divided more evenly between Nixon and McGovern than any other voting group. With Vietnam seemingly over, what will determine their voting in elections to come?

The 1972 election will be remembered as one which revolved in part around the competition for the eighteen-year-old vote. Strangely, though, none of the politicians and neither party really addressed itself to the economic problems of this "entry generation."

Nor is the record of 1972 particularly encouraging. Available government statistics present a mixed picture. At the year's end the unemployment rate for male teen-agers was 14 percent, more than twice the unemployment rate for the country; and for teen-age black males it was 28 percent.

Beyond that, these statistics do not show how many youths were turned down repeatedly not only because of color but for the length of their hair; how many other youths were relegated to jobs with low seniority or security, and so were tossed out repeatedly; and how many others were locked out of work and returned to school.

Some youths weren't given the chance to "shape up" even when they were prepared to. An eighteen-year-old in West Covina, California, recalled, "I went to Food Giant with hair down to my shoulders. I had the experience. I'd bagged at a liquor store and worked as cashier. But the guy told me, 'I don't like your long hair.'

"I was ready to turn establishment to get work," the youth went on. "So I had my hair cut practically bald. The next day when I went back to Food Giant, this same guy said, 'Sorry, we don't have any openings.' It made me so mad. There I was scalped and still no job.

"I've cut my hair five times to get work," he added. "I've given up looking."

The wife of a California longshoreman said, "When our boy got out of service he went from one job to another. Every place there were layoffs, and he was the first to go. After four years, he finally got steady work driving a bus for the city."

Under the prevailing seniority system, younger workers are the first to be laid off if any slowdowns occur. Many face years of uncertain employment before they can count on having a steady job.

Another critical divider that resulted from Nixon's priorities was the sorting of workers into inflation-minus occupations, where salaries failed dismally to keep up with rising living costs, and inflation-plus occupations, where salaries kept rising well above prices.

The inequality of rewards was often astounding and not envisioned in Christopher Jenck's study *Inequality*. Being on a cost-plus contract, for example, paid far better than teaching.

Near Baltimore, a twenty-one-year-old electronics technician—the son of a construction worker—pointed to a new car and motorcycle which he had been able to buy after only three months on his new job.

"While I was in the Navy I thought I'd vote for McGovern," he recalled. "But he wants to cut these defense contracts. I just got hired, so I'd be one of the first to go.

"They used to say when a Republican gets in you're in for hard times," he continued, "but the Republicans haven't hurt me."

In contrast, near York, Pennsylvania, the twenty-year-old wife of an elementary-school teacher protested, "I'm always coming home angry from the grocery store.

"When my husband started teaching, he was supposed to get a raise in September," she went on, "but they took it back in October. We didn't get a regular pay check until January."

Her father, a lifelong Republican, was a state policeman who "keeps hassling me about McGovern being a Communist. But my husband and I are going for McGovern."

She continued, "When my husband graduated as a teacher, the only job he could get was at Burger Chef. We have friends who still don't have teaching jobs. One sent in ninety applications, and he can't even get an interview.

"There are more people out of work and doing work they don't like to since Nixon's been in. Let people do jobs that improve the country. Don't spend so much money on foreign affairs," she urged. "Increase money for education, that's really important. Teachers are so underpaid."

Both of these interviews brought voting shifts from family tradition—the teacher's wife turning Democratic, the electronics worker going Republican—evidence of how strong are the vote-changing powers of a managed economy.

Still other youths were kept out of work by the increased use of overtime that developed during the year. This was somewhat ironic. Making jobs was the professed aim of the Job Development Act, which was passed in August 1971 as part of the wage-price freeze; that was also the reason given for lifting the 7 percent excise tax on automobiles. This purpose was forgotten when auto companies and other industries put people on overtime. By election eve motor-vehicle workers were averaging five and a half overtime hours each week.

Overtime was also a way of improving statistics on the government's cost-of-living performance. The Council of Economic Advisers was able to report that real earnings of factory workers were going up faster than the cost of living.

An Akron, Ohio, youth, when first interviewed in the spring of 1972, told how "I went down the yellow pages and telephoned eighty-one different companies for a job of any kind. Only seven would even take applications."

Reinterviewed a week before the election, he was still

looking for work. "I used to think if you were black you could get a job," he recalled, "but things are so bad I don't even think that helps any more.

"You walk into a company, and they show you the layoff applications they have," he explained. "They have to call all those guys back first, so they won't even talk to me."

What angered him most was that some companies had gone on overtime instead of hiring young people.

"They're getting overtime at the tire plant where my dad works," he protested. "I asked my dad, 'Why won't they hire young guys if there's enough work to give people overtime?' My dad says it's cheaper for the company to pay overtime than to hire somebody new. I don't understand why.

"I'll vote for McGovern because things can't get any worse," he explained. "I don't have a job, so McGovern couldn't hurt me."

Among adults who backed Hubert Humphrey in 1968 and were shifting for Nixon, only one in fifteen was doing worse financially than a year ago. Of those sticking with McGovern, a third said they were worse off.

The few blacks interviewed who swung to Nixon were also better off financially. A laundry supervisor in Seat Pleasant, Maryland, a Humphrey supporter in 1968, said enthusiastically, "Our business is beautiful and getting even better. I'm twenty-six years old and this is my house. It's a great feeling to own something rather than rent it.

"I'll stick with Nixon," he went on. "No one man can do everything. I worked hard and I made it. If you have gumption and ambition you'll do okay."

Among the 1968 supporters of George Wallace, Nixon fared worst with those dissatisfied economically. The big Wallaceite swing to the Republicans came from those who were either satisfied economically or who felt, "Nixon's kept things quiet," or "He hasn't given in to the colored like the Democrats did."

In Fort Worth two workers living across from each other were shifting in opposite political directions.

A twenty-four-year-old non-union electrician was going from Humphrey to Nixon. His company was building the Fort Worth airport.

"This summer we worked eighty hours a week," he explained. "There are only four of us; no new employees were put on. I got a raise after one year; just before the freeze was announced."

He had gone to college and had thought of being a teacher. "But," he explained, "if I were a teacher, I might find myself with a class of colored children. I wouldn't want to be with them."

He hadn't been drafted, but felt, "We ought to go in and clean it up. Show we're a world power. Fight it like a war, do whatever it takes."

He was a "hard-liner" in regard to drugs and capital punishment: "Marijuana is against the law and should be a felony."

On capital punishment he said, "I'd have public hangings and executions. When they hung horse thieves, that stopped them."

Across the street an aerospace toolmaker who had voted for Nixon in 1968 began by saying, "I've been undecided, but I'll give McGovern a chance. I know he can't keep all those promises, but I want a change."

He went on, "I'm fifty-five and may be out of a job soon. The company is laying off men with twenty years seniority. Pretty soon they'll reach me.

"Our union contract raise was negotiated three years ago," he continued, "but it's still being held up.

"With prices and taxes so high, a man can't save any

more. It looks like that's the way they want it, so you won't
have anything left when you go on social security."

2. As the Career Is Bent

"Fire the oldies."

"Get rid of all computers and machines that do away with
jobs."

"Shoot everyone over forty."

"Make jobs to clean up the environment."

"Have more undiscriminating unions."

Those were some of the more typical suggestions offered
by a senior class at Palisades High School in Bucks County,
Pennsylvania, when asked what should be done to make more
jobs for young people.

The remarks revealed how intense are the anxieties of the
young over whether there will be enough jobs, and also how
sharp is their push-them-out conflict with older workers and
their hunger for the creation of new work opportunities.

Currently this new youth generation seems quite fluid
politically. Party loyalties are not strongly held. In 1972 a
fourth to a third of them voted differently from their parents.

Many youths are still not fully reconciled to the two-party
system. A sophomore at Ohio State, when asked for an example
of an unpatriotic action, replied quite seriously, "Voting a
straight ticket without caring who is on it."

My interviewing, though, indicates that the key influence
deciding their future political loyalties is likely to be the job
opportunities that are open—or closed—to them. They will
identify with the party which best serves their own career or
work interests.

Repeatedly during the campaign I was impressed by how
quickly these youths adjusted their political feelings to their
economic situation. Even twins divided that way.

In one Los Angeles suburb a welder's wife talked with pleasure and sorrow of her twenty-year-old sons.

For a time both had favored McGovern; then only one did. The son who turned to Nixon had been trained in his father's shop as a welder and was accepted into the union, which, the mother explained, "means he is making good wages and is secure."

The other twin had worked as a carpenter but couldn't pass the union test. "He was always more opposed to the war," recalled his mother. "He's left for Hawaii. I don't think he'll ever change his feelings about Nixon."

The wife of a machinist in York recalled, "I wanted my nineteen-year-old boy to register, but he just didn't care to vote. He tried and tried to find work, but jobs are so hard to get for kids out of high school. He finally gave up and enlisted in the Seabees."

Her older son, twenty-three, had been for McGovern at one time. "He used to build swimming pools," she explained, "but there was no union and the pay wasn't good.

"He just got this new job as a toolmaker, and he'll get into the union in six more weeks. Now he says he's voting for Nixon."

For many of these youthful workers this pro-Nixon vote marked a historic break from the Democratic tradition of worker families generally opposing Republicans as the party of the bosses.

In the process these young workers became a quite conservative force. They expressed overwhelming support for the President's war policy and our staying in Vietnam. They opposed defense cuts by margins of six to one, often arguing, "Let's face it, our economy needs a war to make jobs."

Although doing well economically, they protested angrily against the taxes taken out of their wages. More than two-thirds of those interviewed wanted to cut welfare. One typical reaction was voiced by the wife of a Kenosha County, Wisconsin, deputy sheriff when she exploded, "It makes me mad when we're working hard to buy a house and we have to pay for people living off welfare."

In contrast, those youths who had not yet entered the economy urged some shift in the country's priorities, usually to "cut down on war and defense" and "use the money to improve the United States."

This desire dominated the thinking of the high-school seniors in Bucks County, who were mainly of working-class and rural origins, of many pro-Nixon youths in college, and, strongest of all, of liberal-arts collegians who were supporting McGovern.

On the campuses the sense of career interest actually sharpened as the campaign progressed. After the summer many students had returned to school in September with sad tales of liberal-arts graduates "frying hamburgers for a living," of "art majors refinishing furniture," of "biology majors who couldn't find even lab work," of how "really rough it is getting a teacher's job."

For them the needed action was to "cut down on the military and spend more on domestic problems."

Anti-war resentments, in short, which had been eased somewhat by the lifting of draft fears, were revived with a new cutting edge of career and economic dissatisfactions.

On the eight campuses where the interviewing was done, a fourth of the first voters with Republican parents were swinging to McGovern.

At Farmingdale, Long Island, a sophomore majoring in data processing explained, "My field is slowly closing. I'm just about getting in underneath a closed door."

He urged, "Stop making bombs. Spend more on domestic areas like education."

"If you want to teach art like I do you're locked out. The jobs are going to accountants, industry, and the trades," protested one twenty-three-year-old at California State in Long Beach.

"I don't talk politics with my parents any more," he explained. "They're diehard Republicans and win-the-war types. I'm for McGovern to get out of the war and put the money into education and the arts and the cities.

"The economy has to be revamped," he went on. "The way it's set up now, we need defense spending. But we could put the money into transportation and pollution control to put people to work."

Both Nixon and McGovern youths seemed to agree on where government spending should be expanded—on pollution control, mass transit, education, medical research, and aid to cities.

This clash with Nixon's priorities was even stronger among the high-school seniors in Bucks County, a normally Republican area. More than three-fourths of the seniors there proposed cutting defense and foreign aid. Anti-pollution was the activity named most often for increased spending.

The sharpest point of student disagreement over priorities came with welfare. While most McGovernites opposed cuts in welfare spending, Nixonites were three to one in favor of cutting welfare.

Young Nixonites of worker background were carriers of even stronger racial resentments. Asked whether colored people were pushing too fast, too slow, or about right, half of them responded, "Too fast," Nixon was widely praised for "leaving racial problems alone."

It was intriguing to note how closely the career choice of a student matched up with how he wanted government spending changed. An aspiring policeman, casting his first vote for

Nixon, wanted to "reduce defense and put more into crime prevention and drugs."

A lawyer's son from Richmond, Virginia, also a Republican, talked of working in a hospital clinic at guidance counseling and mental hygiene. He wanted spending increased on medical research and education.

Many career choices were aimed at working on the problems facing the country.

A sophomore at Hofstra who intended to be a translator recalled, "I did volunteer social work last summer. They need more translators, but won't hire enough. It's a shame, because I saw people come back every week with the same problem because there weren't people there to explain what to do.

"We definitely should switch our priorities from foreign to domestic problems."

A sophomore at Purdue who planned on teaching in an all-black high school in New Orleans was angry that "Nixon has undone all the progressive programs of the Democrats, like the poverty programs and Teachers Corps.

"We've got to cut defense and put more into education and into the cities to get rid of slums. Spend more on rehabilitating and training minority groups like OEO did."

3. How Tight a Ship?

Perhaps the most troubling aspect of the future that Nixon has been organizing for America is how tight a ship he wants to run, with so little shared time and shared experience for the many conflicts already on board.

Much of what the President did in his first four years had to be a response to forces already locked in passionate conflict. His choices were limited, necessitating difficult decisions.

But are we moving toward reconciliation or a widening cleavage? Let us look briefly at some of the more important cleavages.

Confidence between civilians and the military was deteriorating long before Nixon took office. Yet as late as 1966, of the college students interviewed, 61 percent opposed the idea of replacing the draft with a volunteer army. Their general feeling was that "it's all right for a street fight but not for a nation's defense."

By 1971, though, a dragging war had caused a striking change in feeling. Nearly 60 percent of those interviewed favored a volunteer army in place of the draft, although only a tiny minority was willing to volunteer themselves.

Intense distrust of "militarism" was voiced even by those who wanted a volunteer army. A junior in computer programming at Ohio State confessed, "I like the idea of a volunteer army right now because of my lottery number, but I might be sorry later. It puts a lot of power in the army. You'd get hard-core, blow-people-up types in there."

At the University of Pittsburgh, a pro-Nixon law student feared, "It will establish a separate group in society who have all the weapons and who are loyal to its leaders. There'd be a possibility of a military coup."

Ending the draft quieted campus discontent over the war, but it may have deepened distrust of "the military."

Nixon's 1974 budget, as we have seen, threatens to institutionalize military-civilian hostility, by virtually organizing a confrontation between defense expenditures and cuts in social programs.

Turning to racial relations, here again the dominant trend is running toward sharper separation, as against shared experience. This also was happening before Nixon became president. A crude sort of economic lockout for many blacks may be developing, as more and more jobs are moved out of the inner cities to the suburbs. Nothing in evidence suggests that this threat will correct itself.

In the South some racial progress is taking place. Among

young people, conflicting trends show up. In at least four cities
—Baltimore, Fort Worth, Philadelphia, and Lodi, New Jersey
—white youths volunteered that they had picked jobs and
unions where "I wouldn't have to work with colored."

Other white youths—including pro-Republicans—want
to work on the problems of the cities, teaching in black schools
or working in the slums. The government's concept of priorities should be broadened to encourage those who want to work
on the problems of their country.

The blacks, more than any other voting group interviewed, urged, "Stop the junkies," and "Cut down on drug
abuse." Some proposed, "Break all trade relations with countries exporting dope into the United States."

Another high-priority desire called for "more housing that
poorer families can afford to buy," as opposed to "projects."

With black youths the sense of "alienation" is particularly
strong. Asked how they felt about eighteen-year-olds being able
to vote, nearly a third of those interviewed said they did not
intend to vote. Of these, nearly half were undecided on the
career or kind of work they wanted to pursue. Another third
of these non-voters talked of going into social work, with most
of them saying, "I'd like to work only with blacks."

Young blacks who had chosen careers which put them in
contact with whites were generally favorable to integration,
and also more likely to vote than those turned off on integration.

Sometimes black militancy shows a curious face. At the
University of Maryland, a black coed was asked what she
thought about whites and Negroes going to school together.
She replied, "I'd kill off all whites except five."

"Who are these five whites?" she was asked.

She named a roommate and four persons who had helped
her get into college. These were the only white persons whom

she knew personally. Presumably, her figure of five whites worth sparing would be higher if she knew more of them.

Part of the lack of work for young people—white and black, including Vietnam veterans—can be attributed to neglect through statistics by the economic managers, who have been trying to build a case for accepting higher unemployment.

The extent to which the entry generation is left out of the economy is a measure of how stable or upsetting a force they will be for the future.

The importance of opening wider work opportunites was underscored by some interviewing of young people on patriotism. One question put to them was, "What would you consider a patriotic action?"

It was surprising how many youths replied, "Doing something that is good for the country."

Other responses equated patiotism with "not destroying the environment" or "improving relations among people and subduing conflict." An "unpatriotic action" was often descibed as "anything that harms others."

Giving young people the opportunity to work on the problems of the country would constitute common ground on which a new pride and confidence in oneself and the country could be built.

"Improve the environment" stands out as the activity chosen for more government spending by young people of varied political feelings—by high-school seniors in a Republican area of Pennsylvania, by pro-Nixon and pro-McGovern college students.

Adults also share this desire. They talk of the work that can be done to "make our cities liveable" or to clean up the air as an answer to the argument that "the country needs a war to prosper." Often it is suggested as a way of providing jobs for people on welfare.

For young people this spur to better the environment has deep psychological roots. A peculiar streak of pessimism touches much of this Vietnam generation. When asked how many children they will have, almost always they reply, "Not more than two and maybe only one." The reasons given stress how overcrowded they feel the world has become: "Too many people being born." . . . "There are too many autos." . . . "Too many people increases the chance of war." . . . "We won't have the resources for our children."

At Carnegie Tech, a sophomore in chemical engineering cited this experience:

"We live in the Allison Park section of Pittsburgh, and Pine Creek runs through our back yard. I spent $100 to clean up the creek. Scouts and kids in the neighborhood all helped out. We carried all the garbage and debris out and everybody contributed.

"Then one of the plants up the creek went on strike and closed down their filtering system," he went on. "Now the creek is all rust-colored again."

Of course, there are technical and economic problems to be overcome, but that has its advantage. They are difficulties which open opportunities for Americans to work together.

Reconciliation is also a family matter, not a problem of youth alone. Many parents have been waiting for the war's end hoping that it would remove tensions that threatened to break apart their families or even bring back a son or daughter who has left home.

In one Washington suburb a post-office worker supported the Vietnam war some years ago but had come around to opposing it. When I reinterviewed him, he wanted us to pull out. He explained that as the war had dragged on, issues erupted that separated him from his two sons, seventeen and twenty-one. He hoped an end to the war would end the family conflict.

"When my oldest boy was in high school," the father recalled, "he was a diehard segregationist like I am. In college he became one of these liberals and thinks everything that is wrong with Negroes is the white man's fault.

"I like to think my boy doesn't use drugs," the father went on. "I know he says some of the sentences for having marijuana are too stiff. Maybe it ought to be legalized so they don't go on to harder stuff."

The dread that one's own child may become addicted is probably the biggest family nightmare in the country. How parents are trying to deal with this problem yields some insights into the relationship of individualism and government.

Spiro Agnew and others blamed addiction on a permissive society, to be corrected by a return to discipline.

Many parents are making zealous efforts to educate their children or to stiffen their moral fiber so their sons or daughters will reject the use of drugs. But generally these same parents want the government to take any action that may curb drug use. No one is prepared to rely on what he can do as an individual with his children.

Here are a few examples of what parents have been doing to prevent their kids from becoming drug addicts:

"We don't let our children take any pills," explained a twenty-eight-year-old sales engineer in Virginia. "You have to talk to them early before they start school. Tell them how bad drugs are the same time you tell them big snakes are bad."

When an Iowa farm wife was asked why she felt her sons would not take drugs, she replied, "We've turned our farm into a profit-sharing enterprise to give them a sense of self-reliance. Every summer we vacation together in Canada."

A bread salesman's wife said, "I've told my children never to accept pills or candy or drinks from anybody, not even your teacher or the school nurse."

Yet however firmly these parents act or talk, they cannot

be sure their efforts will work. Nor will they be given the answer in one year—nor in ten.

The wife of a Con Ed pipe installer in Astoria, Queens, explained, I'm secretary at the Catholic high school and the drug problem is terrible there. I think I've made my kids afraid of drugs. You can hold on to them and hope and pray while they're in grade school and high school, but my son is going on to college. What do I do now?

"I'm so worried about him. Some days I wish he could grow up all at once. Other days I wish he were younger so I could keep him home longer. What I really want, I guess, is a private island for my family."

Her son was the oldest of six children, from seven to eighteen years old, which meant that five more times—over at least fifteen years—she would have to endure the ordeal of guarding her children against drug pushers in school hallways or at rock festivals in nearby parks.

Addiction is rarely a moral issue for families whose children have taken to drugs or who live in nieghborhoods that are terrorized by the drug traffic. Then these parents become concerned only with action that may work, that may make a difference.

A rising proportion of adults interviewed are coming to question the stiff penalties on the possession of marijuana. More thought is also being given to proposals to "take the profit out of heroin" by setting up clinics where any addict can be treated.

In this country there has never been a rigid or even consistent line marking off what should be left to the individual and what should be undertaken by government. The same person will shift his ideological sights depending on what agitates him. A real-estate salesman in Richmond, Virginia, protested, "The government has too much power. People should vote on anything that affects everyone like school busing."

A bit later he remarked, "We're going to have socialized medicine. No one can pay these medical bills."

Currently there is a quite common feeling through the country that health insurance is a necessity.

This struggle to keep individualism and government in balance has never been absent from American history. One might say, in fact, that this is the essence of the American national character, never to be content with too much government or too much individualism, but to be seeking constantly the balance between them.

The unique quality of our present crisis may lie in just this fact, that the battling has spread to almost every imaginable issue—drugs, abortion, amnesty, the press, capital punishment, wire tapping, Women's Liberation, racial separation and integration, a whole range of economic issues.

These are not impersonal clashes of the law against John Doe but of people against people, of groups of Americans with clashing values who differ over the uses to which government is to be put.

With abortion and capital punishment, the Supreme Court has drawn a line, which some Americans refuse to accept. Certainly no single edict will settle all these controversies; nor is there some single, hard-line attitude that covers all "social issues." How people identify with each of these issues is what seems to shape their reactions.

Persons who supported amnesty, for example, had usually thought of someone close to them—a son or brother—who might have faced the same choice of refusing to serve.

A Maryland school secretary, who was a George Wallace supporter, had a thirteen-year-old son. She said, "They should be given amnesty. I'd want my son to do the same thing. I can't see fighting in that war."

In Tampa, Florida, a loan adjuster's wife who was voting for Nixon explained why she favored amnesty: "I have a one-

year-old son, and I wonder when he grows up will there be
something like Vietnam for him to get killed in. My husband
and I have talked about putting savings bonds aside so we can
go to Canada if there's another war."

Some persons who supported amnesty were for keeping
capital punishment or were strongly prejudiced against blacks.

Currently, it is on the economic front that the stakes are
highest, the battling most intense, and the confusion the great-
est. The stakes are highest because the economy is being used
as the shaping force for the future, which may also explain why
the confusion is so heavy.

Much of President Nixon's attacks on "government"
seems directed to create the impression that government per
se is inefficient. This is simply not true.

My own experience in government was during World
War II, when our government did a magnificent job organizing
to fight and win the equivalent of two great wars—in Europe
and Asia—each half the world apart. Nothing in history mat-
ches the scale of that effort.

During recent years sizable mistakes of private planning
and management have taken place; to wit, the telephone company in misjudging the needs of the New York area, and the
periodic electricity blackouts around the country. The developing energy crisis argues further against any reliance on a philosophy that business in the pursuit of its own profit will surely
arrive at the national interest. To the contrary, we can be
certain that overstimulation of the "private" side of our
economy will generate dislocations and disturbances that a
wise use of government could have anticipated and avoided or
minimized.

In my files is a clipping of a prophetic story written by
Alan L. Otten of the *Wall Street Journal*, back in August
1971, saying that the Nixon administration might come to

regret placing so heavy a reliance for economic recovery on the expansion of auto production. A good part of our $6.8 billion trade deficit reflects increased oil imports; the radios for most automobiles sold in this country are no longer manufactured in the United States.

Money is not government. Without the balancing hand of government, no society, whatever its affluence, can survive.

Chapter *9*

Power through Failure

As WE END this story of our experience with total politics, two ironies should be noted:

First, where Nixon's policies failed, they actually brought an expansion of presidential power.

Second, despite Nixon's rhetoric of tough discipline, a heavy majority of voters interviewed during the compaign— and particularly Nixon supporters—wanted more for themselves.

Slogans such as "self-reliance" and the "work ethic" in White House speeches had the ring of Puritan or Spartan discipline. The President also appealed for greater productivity and a stronger competitive effort to be able to export more and reduce the trade deficit.

American voters did indeed become more competitive

than they were in 1968, but not with any sense of austerity or apparent effect on our balance of payments. Their competitiveness was directed primarily toward their own individual profit and often against other Americans.

After the election these pressures for "still more" continued to be encouraged even while the President was seeking unprecedented powers to conduct trade negotiations around the world. That coupling—to ask for more power while orchestrating higher voter demands—should not strike us as strange in view of the basic contradiction embedded in the Nixon majority. It is a coalition whipped on by fierce economic drives made more difficult to restrain because of an anti-tax, anti-government ideology the President is pushing.

Virtually everything described in earlier chapters will go on—workers on "cost-plus" contracts will remain untroubled about getting overtime pay for "doing nothing" on a Saturday; others envious of medical benefits and food stamps for welfare recipients, want the equivalent for themselves.

Labor unionists who voted for the President will bargain for higher wage guidelines and more "take home" pay after taxes. Business will seek higher profits, also after taxes.

Everyone who can will be pushing for higher and earlier pensions to gain some reassurance against inflation as "a fact of life." The military pay increases already scheduled account for much of the jump in the total defense budget.

Nixon's "tough" anti-spending rhetoric will also persist. For years ahead, though, chronic inflation will remain endemic to our whole world. The real political competition will be over who benefits from how this inflation is manipulated. It is the impact of the President's economic powers as a whole—of tax relief and subsidies as well as spending—that need to be watched. Is the net result greater equity for all? Or, as has held so far, advantage for his political supporters?

The mistakes and political actions of president-managers are likely to give the economy shakes and bounces. Some critics of the economic drama are predicting a flop—that is, a recession—for 1974 which should help the Democrats. President-managers, though, can persist in blunders without great political change. Failures, in fact, could become the means of gaining additional power—as occurred during 1971, when Nixon seemed to be going down to certain defeat.

By the spring of 1971, Nixon's original "game plan" was collapsing. With unemployment at 6 percent, living costs were still climbing by 4.5 percent. Early in May a heavy flow of dollars into Germany warned that a currency crisis might be developing.

Fears that "a depression is coming" were spreading through the country. At the time, I was conducting a seventeen-state survey for *Look* magazine on the effects of lowering the voting age to eighteen. Wherever I interviewed among students, workers, and farmers, Nixon's Vietnam policies were being tied to economic uncertainty. His slow withdrawal from Vietnam was being defended—and attacked—as if his main motivation were economic, not strategic.

At the University of Kentucky, a pre-law student admitted, "I'd like to pull out of Vietnam, but the economy couldn't stand it, which is a hell of a reason for fighting a war."

The counterfire returned, "Too many people are getting rich off this war to end it," or "Pull out now and spend all that Vietnam money here at home."

As people's thinking leaped ahead to 1972, a general expectation developed that economic conditions would be worse next year. An engineer in Minneapolis reflected this reasoning when he asked, "If we can't control unemployment now, how much worse will it get next year when the soldiers come home?"

In staunchly Republican Story County, Iowa, a local banker declared gloomily, "We're already in a depression." Every third Republican interviewed talked of switching from Nixon.

A seventy-one-year-old farmer volunteered, "I've never voted Democrat for president in my life, but I may next year. I lend out some money. At five and a half percent you can sleep. When it's eight percent, you stay awake worrying whether the loans can be paid."

This farmer was ready to vote for "any Democrat except Senator Harold Hughes." He explained, "I had a contract to haul garbage. When Hughes became governor, he passed a law that you had to cook the garbage before you could haul it away. That put me out of business."

When the President announced that he would visit Red China, the overexcited media pictured the move as a brilliant political coup; actually, it proved a political dud.

The Gallup Poll showed no rise in Nixon's popularity. My interviewing revealed sharp opposition.

"Nixon can go there and stay there" was the feeling of one Virginia mother.

A Maryland bank clerk voiced a more typical reaction when he said, "Why doesn't Nixon tend to his own country and forget about everybody else. We have enough problems here."

So deep were fears of economic collapse that voters had stopped listening to the President and to politicians generally. Their dreads had pushed people beyond the reach of slogans, rhetoric, or images. Action was the only message that was communicable.

The wage-price freeze did break the tune-out barrier for Nixon. With it, his economic policies a failure until then, came a spectacular expansion of presidential power.

A Democratic-controlled Congress approved the economic-recovery program Nixon proposed with little change. Congress could have written into law stronger and fairer wage-price controls, as was done during World War II. Congress could also have modified the President's tax incentives to widen the range of economic priorities. Congress did neither. Given what he asked for, Nixon proceeded to use the new job-making and spending powers to restructure the economy according to his priorities.

In starting his second term, Nixon announced a relaxation of Phase III controls as a move back to the "free market." The stock exchange dived; a currency crisis forced a second devaluation of the dollar.

Again the President sought to move from failure to more power, asking for the broadest authority to both raise and lower American tariffs.

It is not easy for Congress or for the party out of office to advance effective economic alternatives to a president-manager.

People may conclude that this is simply another illustration of presidential superiority in dealing with complex administrative matters.

But a deeper question was raised earlier in this book when we examined why, during the primaries, the Democrats were unable to target the many voter discontents against Nixon.

My net conclusion was that the sense of self-interest in the country had become so fragmented that it probably was impossible to develop any single "program"—that term so beloved by Democrats—to deal with these many conflicts.

One might capsule the political challenge posed by the President in this way—it has become smarter politics to favor the many and not try to be fair to all. Effective resistance to this doctrine is needed for Americans to recover their sense of equity and social responsibility.

Technological and economic change has plunged the whole world into turbulent transition. The new structurings are not moving to the "internationalism" of separate nations that was envisioned by Woodrow Wilson or to "One World" in Wendell Willkie's sense. Still, the nation-pieces are being brought together into new groupings. The multinational corporations are speeding the integration of all economies. Simultaneously, new vulnerabilities are being generated by economic change inside countries, as with our growing dependence on oil imports. Given present trends, the Arab countries will be acquiring huge dollar reserves from these oil sales, which could be used to upset any currency stabilization and even to pressure for changes in American policy toward Israel and the Middle East.

Inside this country we are caught up in the same transition. My interviewing revealed a general groping for protection from many uncertainties. Access to secure work, insurance against erosion of savings, the assurance of peace under a controlled nuclear deterrent, protection against crime, stable conditions of racial competition, the political visibility which makes certain that Big Brother government does not forget us—those are some of the pressures and needs that are spurring the voters to want new governmental forms.

In medieval times similar uncertainties brought feudalism into existence. Yet "modern feudalism" is not the term that describes what we are moving toward. No one has the right word for it yet.

As we move into the future, it will help to have some guiding principles. In regard to the powers of the presidency, I would suggest:

First, yield power only in small doses.

With trade negotiations, for example, it would be wiser to take up one part of the problem at a time, have the president-manager come back with the results approved by Congress, and go on from there.

Second, bring all power under the law.

The presidency has become a government in itself. Its inner workings should be regulated by law rather than "executive privilege." Some deliberate ambiguities were left in the Constitution, but not to justify "executive privilege" where corruption is alleged, as with the ITT and Watergate activities.

Third, the managing of our society should be organized to unite this great country as the Constitution provides. Perhaps I should add this final personal note. While in high school, I took part in a city-wide oratorical contest on the Constitution. In writing my speech, I studied the minutes of the Constitutional Convention. That experience left me with a firm faith in our constitutional government, tested repeatedly in later years, which is reflected in all my political writings.

The preamble of the Constitution remains the most relevant language Americans have: ". . . to form a more perfect union, establish justice, insure domestic tranquility, provide for the common defense, promote the general welfare, and secure the blessings of liberty to ourselves and our posterity."

Appendix

Methodology: A Time-Place Machine

1. Voting As a River

FAR MORE IMPORTANT than whether the Republicans or Democrats emerge as the top-dog "majority party" are the *effects* of the raging struggle to realign the parties and gain political control. What will our leaders and clashing interests feel driven to do next to win and hold power? How will they try to rearrange public thinking? To overwhelm or transform our institutions? Where will power and conflict break loose? Where will they be made governable?

Before a stable voting majority comes into being, much of American society will be transformed and the course of American history committed, perhaps irrevocably, for decades to come.

These thoughts were a major theme of a talk I delivered

before the Organization of American Historians at their April 1971 meeting in New Orleans.

The total election of 1972 has given this speech a new timeliness, particularly since it also includes an exposition of why my methodology for interviewing and voting analysis is especially suited for so convulsive and hectic a period of social, economic, and political change.

In the field of public opinion, voting, and political behavior, too heavy a reliance is being placed on one method of inquiry and analysis—the survey interview in a statistical cross-section poll. Competing methodologies are needed if we are to learn from the current turbulence what government and politics in this country really mean.

The invention that I introduced to polling was to do my interviewing and analysis in specific voting precincts, matching interview results with the past vote, in order to report *how much change* had taken place and why.

I first used this precinct approach to cover the 1952 campaign, and that same year on election night on CBS, on the basis of returns from three precincts in Richmond, I said at 8:35 P.M. that Eisenhower had cracked the South, carrying Virginia and Florida, and was on his way to a landslide.*

This precinct approach was later adopted by all the networks, as well as by Louis Harris and Richard Scammon, and still serves as the basis for most election-night projections.

It was always fun on election nights to go up against the computers with my precinct selections, and nearly always I called the outcome first. Far more important than this stunt performance, though, is something not generally appreciated —that the use of voting returns sets up a Time-Place discipline which makes possible an enormously more sensitive kind of

*See the election-night review by Ben H. Bagdikian in the Providence *Journal* on November 5, 1952.

interviewing with a smaller and more economical sample, and which will measure change. Voting returns are available for every locality; the method can be used by any of the many disciplines—historians, political scientists, sociologists, journalists—in one's "home town." What is learned locally would serve as a check upon national polls and those done for the candidates. The competition would improve all polling and could, perhaps most important, strengthen the hands of the voters against the manipulations of the politicians.

Extracts from this speech before the Historians follow. Some sections have been rearranged for a clearer explanation of my methodology. Since the talk was built largely around the results of the 1970 elections, new material that projects the methodology into 1972 is included, as well as some updating comments.

These updating comments are set off in brackets.

"Too much voting research has relied on methods designed to discover how to sell people things. Casting a ballot is indeed a psychological action. But it is a psychological action which cannot be fathomed fully unless placed in a historical time-system. Voting is truly like a river that rises in the past and empties into the future.

"My own approach has been basically historical, being rooted in a continuing analysis of election results and the use of carefully selected precincts as the basis for interviewing. This means going beyond the aggregate data that may be available on a national or county basis and getting down to the smallest unit available—the precinct or town. Until one has worked with election returns on an intimate and continuing basis, it is difficult to appreciate, even to imagine, how rewarding a body of data voting statistics is.

"From voting returns one can construct a kind of time-space machine, with its own built-in radar for locating social change. With this time machine, one is able to wing across the country, matching any and all localities against one another, stopping wherever curiosity suggests a landing to determine why people differ in their political thinking. The time machine can also be used to roam back and forth across the whole of American history.

"This potential reflects, of course, the *fact* that election returns constitute a time-place series, recording how people mark their ballots election after election, place by place. Through the returns one can take any locality and the people living there and relate them to the rest of the nation.

"By following these relationships through a succession of elections, one can spot where political attitudes have changed, where they have not. Even the most nondescript crossroads polling place keeps alive with significance. One's study of the voting of any locality can be further enriched by all of the information available on a geographic basis, census data, local histories, on-the-spot visits.

"This time-machine approach requires its own discipline, to be imposed on our psychological selves. To make sense, *the explanation of the change from one election to the next must fit what happened in areas which shifted their vote* in contrast to those which did not change.

"That rule would seem axiomatic, and yet it has been ignored repeatedly by historians, journalists, politicians, and social scientists in explaining elections.

"As one example, there is the famous 'Rum, Romanism, and Rebellion' remark which history credits with defeating James G. Blaine in 1884. An unpublished analysis of mine reveals that this remark could not have cost Blaine the election. In New York State, Blaine was defeated not by Catholics and wets, but by Protestant drys and better-income Republicans. A ward-by-ward analysis showed that Blaine gained votes over

1880 in the Irish sections of New York City, while dropping in the highest Republican wards.

"This rule of explaining the election by where the vote changed is not easy to apply in reconstructing elections long past, but it remains a standard that researchers should strive for.* There is no good reason, however, why this rule cannot be applied to all current elections, combining analysis of the vote with interviewing.

"Harry Truman's surprising victory in 1948 offers a good illustration. Pollsters still cling to the claim that their polls went wrong because of voter shifts during the last days of the campaign. This is difficult to accept when one studies the vote in detail. In quite a number of areas, both rural and urban, Truman ran well ahead of Franklin Roosevelt's showing in 1944 and 1940.

"Everywhere these gains are found in quite similar areas which broke heavily against Roosevelt between 1936 and 1940. Essentially what happened was that the isolationist voters, who had gone against Roosevelt because of World War II, returned to the Democratic Party in 1948. Mainly, they were of German, Irish, and Italian descent, including many supporters or William Lemke, who was Father Coughlin's presidential candidate in 1936. Until this evidence was set forth in my "Future of American Politics," none of the polls even asked voters their nationality background.

"The shifting pattern of the isolationist voter also points to a truly unique characteristic of voting. No individual can be said really to vote for the first time. Always he is part of a stream of conditioning that has shaped the political loyalties

*See Lee Benson's "Research Problems in American Political Historiography," in Mirra Komarovsky's *Common Frontiers of the Social Sciences.* The best results will be obtained when the analysis is carried down to wards and towns and precincts, where available.

and antagonisms of his family, his community, the varied groupings to which the voter belongs. When these loyalties do break, they often behave like streams that flow underground, out of sight for a time, only to surface anew, an election or several elections later, as in 1948. As a result, each subsequent election casts new light on the elections that have gone before.

"That has been the basic discipline I have held to in all my election surveys. Always it has been the *change* from one election to the next that I have tried to understand and report.

"In my interviewing I probe thoroughly for the motivations of any voter who indicates he is likely to shift from how he voted in the past.

"Automatically this becomes a probing of history as well. Before going into any precinct, I check its past voting history up to the election at hand. My interviewing is then guided to determine how and why that voting stream will move in the current election. Will the stream flow on untroubled, break out of its channel in anger, just seep a little? Are old loyalties reasserting themselves or breaking more strongly? Working in this fashion, one gets the sense of watching the future while it happens.

"Concentrating on change also forced me to develop techniques for separating one voting influence from another. Which of the varied factors that put pressure upon a voter make him change? Which hold other voters firm? Here again the past voting returns sensitize one in advance to the voter conflicts that can be expected in each specific precinct." [To illustrate this approach, let us examine one of the decisive issues of 1972—racial polarization—in an earlier stage.]

2. The New Conservatism

"One advantage in basing political analysis and interviewing on election returns is that it makes it possible to approximate accurately when a trend of voting change began and how it developed in successive elections.

"Take James Buckley's 1970 victory in New York State as the first Conservative Party senator in the country. It is always tempting to attribute such a happening to headlined events at the time. If one examines Buckley's vote, it plainly was a projection of the racial polarization that had been intensifying inside New York City since the 1966 referendum on the civilian review board.

"The territorial pattern of this polarization for New York and other northern cities is described in *The Hidden Crisis in American Politics* (pp. 127–236).

"So marked was this polarizing spread that we decided to use it as the basis for our 1970 interviewing for both governor and senator.

"A ladder-like scaling of nine predominantly white precincts—three at each of three different levels of voter feeling —was constructed for particularly intensive interviewing. At one end were election precincts that had shown strong resentments against both the civilian review board and Mayor Lindsay, but which favored Richard Nixon. In these areas Rockefeller was expected to improve his vote over 1966 and Buckley to draw his heaviest support.

"At the other end of the scale, where Buckley and Rockefeller were expected to fare poorly, were three precincts which voted to keep the civilian review board, were high for Lindsay, and low for Nixon. In between were precincts which scaled around the city average in these elections.

"As a safeguard, we also interviewed in sixteen other neighborhoods scattered through the whole city, so as not to miss some important development that might not be caught in our "intensive" precincts.

"In pre-1970 elections, the nine precincts chosen for intensive interviewing averaged out at 4 to 6 percent more Republican than the whole city.

"In the 1970 voting they held this same relationship to the city, giving Governor Rockefeller 52 percent, or 5 percent higher than did the whole city, and Buckley 42 percent, or 6 percent above his city average.

"Such statistical exactness requires some element of good fortune, of course. Still, this scaling should demonstrate that election returns can be employed to yield projections as mathematically precise as with any method of sampling. Even the most quantitative heart would find unexpected delights in the use of voting returns."

[But statistical projection has never been my interviewing goal. My prime concern has been always to develop as rich an understanding as possible of the vote change taking place.

A series of questions was framed to determine what "conservatism" and "liberalism" meant to two antagonistic groups —the pro-Buckley and anti-Buckley voters.

The analysis which follows has a special appeal in that it sounds like a preview of Nixon's 1972 campaign, with the identical emphasis on the "work ethic" linked to welfare angers.]

"When Buckley supporters were asked what conservatism meant to them, three themes were emphasized most often.

" 'Get people off welfare.'

"they're taxing us to death.'

"we worked ourselves up from nothing.'

"Usually these protests were voiced in terms that justified the efforts of people bent upon lifting themselves as individuals and scornful of using the government to improve society generally. Often, disparaging remarks about blacks would be added.

"I've worked every day of my life and I've never asked for anything,' protested a customers clerk in Manhattan. 'The colored want everything for nothing.'

"A moving man in Brooklyn complained, 'Let them clean the streets for a couple of bucks an hour. Don't give healthy people money.'

"Protested one Brooklyn telephone operator, 'My husband has two jobs. I have three kids and I still work. But we're not on welfare.'

"It would be going too far to label these anti-tax and anti-government angers as a revival of the social Darwinism of the 1890s. Many of these Buckleyites favored the expansion of Medicare. Still, there was an 'every man for himself' and a 'let them shape up' tone to their repeated assertions of 'no one gave us anything for nothing.'

"In opposing higher taxes and government programs with such vehemence, they were fighting to shake free of unwanted social burdens, to hold on to their own earnings, hoping the costs of mounting welfare loads and inflation would fall on someone else.

"Resentments against higher taxes were also expressed in the high Lindsay and low Buckley precincts, but here voters talked of how 'we must change society.' Better education was often cited as the 'key to all our problems.' There was much lamenting that 'everything goes for the military' diverting funds from 'the programs' that these voters felt were needed to deal with the city's problems.

"In Buckley neighborhoods the term "rehabilitation" brought snorts of contempt and demands for stiffer punishment rather than better education. Many volunteered, 'Bring back capital punishment,' often adding, 'There are cops in my family.'

"Their praise of the 'neighborhood school' and opposition to the busing of school children reflected a belief that this was an effective way of excluding nearly all blacks from their neighborhoods.

[My talk before the Historians also contained an observation which applied to our 1972 interviewing as well—that anti-tax advocates are not as anti-government as is generally believed in terms of what government services they expect.]

"The Buckley supporters are *not as deeply anti-govern-ment* as patron Saint Bill would have us believe. Despite the vehemence of their anti-tax protestations, they do not want important government services reduced. Most Buckley voters we interviewed would expand Medicare, as already noted. They wanted more frequent garbage collections and 'a stop to pollution'; many felt that New York City's subways should be not only safe but that the cars should be air-conditioned.

"The Buckleyites who belong to labor unions defend them strongly, primarily for the specific benefits that union membership gives. They resent suggestions that unions be opened wider to black membership. In short, they do not favor an end to the benefits of government or union action, as long as they can be at the head of the line in receiving those benefits."

[How I summed up the political significance of the Buck-ley vote would also apply to 1972.]

"This intensification of economic individualism coupled with racial polarization points to what I believe is becoming the central conflict in the current battling to realign our political parties. The contrast with how the Roosevelt coalition was brought together is striking. In establishing the Democrats as the normal majority party, Roosevelt did not root out the racial and religious antagonisms that had divided blacks and whites or Protestants and Catholics. What Roosevelt did was to tem-per, subdue, repress these tensions under a stronger, Depres-sion-born sense of common economic purpose, tied to the advancement of trade unionism and benevolent government action.

"The Buckley conservatives seem to be carriers of economic pressures and drives which would tear apart the sense of common economic purpose between blacks and whites and even between clashing white elements."

[At that time, our interviewing showed gains for Nixon over 1968. One might also note that our survey includes the standard questions on the background characteristics of the voters, plus tabulations on how the persons interviewed felt about the Vietnam war and the economy.

Further extracts from the Historians talk follow:]

"Contrary to advance publicity, the Buckley supporters were not mainly hard-hats or blue-collar workers. More than two-thirds of those we interviewed were white-collar employees, sundry salesmen, government employees (often retired), second-level Wall Street types, and company executives. Only about a third were construction workers, truck drivers, cargo handlers, or factory hands.

"Four of every five policemen interviewed went for Buckley. Nearly 70 percent of his backing was Catholic. His appeal was particularly heavy among voters of German, Irish, and, even more so, Italian descent. Of these Buckley supporters, 59 percent were long-term Republicans. Another 14 percent were Democrats who said they would remain Democratic for president in 1972. Four percent had gone for George Wallace in 1968; they intended to divide evenly between the Democrats and Republicans in 1972. The remaining 23 percent could be looked on as potential party switchers.

"Of these, 17 percent had voted for both John Kennedy and Lyndon Johnson, shifted to Nixon, and wanted Nixon re-elected.

"An additional 6 percent had gone for Hubert Humphrey in 1968 but said they would switch to Nixon in 1972.

"The pulls to Nixon mainly reflected feelings on the war, racial and welfare resentments, and—the only word that fits—

a hatred of Mayor John Lindsay. Even women broke into profanity at the mention of Lindsay's name.

"Typical comments ran, 'He turned New York into a welfare city' or 'He steps on everyone to help the colored.'

"Asked how they felt about Nixon's handling of the war, 88 percent of the Buckley voters voiced approval; better than 90 percent favored Nixon's desire to limit integration to 'the neighborhood school.' On Nixon's handling of the economy, though, his support dropped to 58 percent. Only 37 percent thought it would be better for the economy to have Republicans control Congress.

TABLE 2

Would It Be Better for the Economy if the Democrats or Republicans Controlled Congress?

VOTERS FOR:	DEMOCRATS	REPUBLICANS	NO DIFFERENCE
Buckley	28%	37%	35%
Ottinger	69	12	19
Goodell	62	14	24

"On the war one should not leap to the conclusion that all Buckleyites are so-called hawks. Elsewhere I have pointed out why efforts to classify voters as hawks or doves are deceptive.*

"The bird that has truly symbolized American war opinion has been neither the dove nor the hawk but the albatross.

"One interview question ran: 'What should we do now in Vietnam—pull out, step up the fighting, or go along the way we are?'

"Roughly 40 percent of the Buckley supporters replied, 'Pull out,' while only 21 percent wanted the fighting stepped up. Buckleyite sentiment for escalation was far higher, though

*See *The Hidden Crisis in American Politics*, pp. 260–61.

(see Table 3), than with supporters of Senator Charles Goodell or Ottinger.

TABLE 3
What Should U.S. Do in Vietnam?

VOTERS FOR:	STEP UP FIGHTING	PULL OUT	SAME AS NOW	STEP UP OR PULL OUT (VOLUNTEERED)
Buckley	21%	41%	35%	3%
Ottinger	7	72	18	3
Goodell	0	81	17	2

"When Tables 2 and 3 are compared, one is struck by how similar were the views of the Ottinger and Goodell voters. Spiro Agnew swung few votes to Buckley. His contribution to the Conservative cause lay in infuriating the 'liberals' into voting for Goodell, splitting the 'Liberal-Democratic' vote."

[During the 1972 campaign we went back into some of these same New York City precincts to determine whether tensions were easing or being intensified. Our reinterviews with many of the same families are reported in Chapter Three.

One note: Whenever we go into a neighborhood that has been covered before, our rule is to pick up new interviews as well, to determine the trend of voter change independently of the persons talked to in previous elections.

Reinterviews are particularly valuable in yielding a keener sense of the trend of change being studied, even to what could halt or reverse this trend.

In one pro-Buckley precinct in Queens, where we interviewed in both 1970 and 1972, the wife of a utilities worker volunteered these comments in explaining why she had turned toward "conservatism."

"I wanted Lindsay out so bad in 1969," she recalled, "and I wanted to vote conservative because Lindsay is liberal and I'm the opposite. But I stood in that voting booth and couldn't get my little finger to press the Conservative button, so I voted for Procaccino.

"But I voted for Senator Buckley. I'm sorry I didn't start voting Conservative long before that."

Until 1968 she had never gone Republican for president. She intended to go for Nixon's re-election.

Asked about the two parties, she replied, "I'm a Democrat but I'm a conservative. If the Democrats stand for what I stand for, they get my vote. But if not, sorry, Charlie.

"I call myself conservative, but I'm not real conservative. We couldn't have everything strictly conservative, because the poor people would starve and they should be helped. If my kids were starving, I might rob a store so my kids could eat."

She was also critical of companies going abroad and of "the rich" not paying their share of taxes. "If we allow big business to go to Europe for cheap labor," she suggested, "they should at least have their tax loopholes taken away and make 'em pay.

"If the rich paid the same taxes we do, our taxes would go down a whole lot. Everybody should pay a certain percent of what they make. I don't believe in brackets because it kills incentive. If you're willing to work to make more money, they shouldn't tax you a higher rate for making more.

"The way it is now," she went on, "people have to go to their broker in September to find out if it's worth working any more overtime for the next three months because it might all go for taxes."

Such reinterviews yield a double crop—the intimate detail of the whole person is retained, with her many shadings and nuances of feeling; yet she also represents the pattern of voting change in her precinct and much of the city.

One might liken it to going back to the same river and

lowering a bucket in precisely the same place to determine how the water sample has changed.

Without previous interviews, we often would not realize that voters had changed their feelings from earlier years. This year in Akron and Barberton, Ohio, we caught the fact that attitudes on Vietnam had shifted with economic adversity. Having spotted this tie-in between economic grievance and opposition to the war, we would check it specifically in our interviewing through the rest of the country.

Sometimes the same area will be sampled two or three times during a campaign, to check how a particular voter conflict is being resolved. In Warren, Michigan, economic angers undercut anti-busing sentiment during the spring, but not in July, when the economy had lifted.

By employing these same methods in selected southern precincts, we could also determine how "conservatism" in northern areas differed from the "conservatism" developing in Dixie.

In the North, the "new conservatism" seemed mainly a revolt against an overloaded sense of social responsibility, caused largely by the migration of blacks from the rural South. In the South, this "conservatism" was a mixture of anti-Negro feeling plus a hunger for acquisitive gain that resembled the drive of a society emerging from an earlier poverty, proudly flexing its new economic muscle, but still unwilling to accept any sizable welfare burden.

One revealing anecdote was included in the Historians speech.]

"The Republican committeeman in a suburban Nashville precinct was a thirty-seven-year-old doctor, one of thirteen children from Georgia. His father, a photographer, had never paid much attention to politics, rarely bothering to vote.

"For this young doctor, though, politics meant an ideological cleavage as sharp as a scalpel. Asked what the parties stood for, he replied, 'I'm more of a Republican—a conservative. The Republicans are for people with initiative and drive. The Democrats are for people who lack these qualities.

" 'The income tax,' he went on, 'penalizes initiative instead of rewarding it. Welfare should stop rewarding husbands who desert their families. Make them work.'

"His wife was a nurse; they had been at medical school together. When I asked how she felt about school integration, she replied, 'It's just a plot to disrupt our families.'

"The poverty this doctor had been raised in had fueled him with a fierce, competitive drive which left little room for anyone who couldn't make it the hard way.

"Particularly impressive was the fact that the doctor was one of thirteen children. When I got back to Washington, I checked the size of white families in the South during the 1940s. Roughly 35 percent of them had six or more children, while 20 percent had eight or more children.

"In both the South and the North we are witnessing an upsurge of a militant economic individualism that tends to separate itself from the black population."

[In the Richmond, Virginia, area we scaled all precincts by their vote for Nixon, Wallace, and Humphrey in 1968, and then mapped them geographically in the city and in suburban Henrico and Chesterfield counties. The high Republican, low Wallace precincts clustered to the west, while the high Wallace precincts were north, east, and south of the city.*

On checking the 1969 election for governor, we found that the vote for Republican Linwood Holton was uniformly high in the Richmond area, but noted a sharp break in the voting for lieutenant governor, with the high Wallace pre-

*For a more detailed analysis of the Richmond area, see *The Hidden Crisis in American Politics*, pp. 146–55.

cincts going for the Democrat, J. Sargent Reynolds, who carried the state. This vote gave us a scaling of the latent pro-Democratic strength among the Wallace supporters.

"On this basis we chose Broad Rock, then in Chesterfield County and later annexed to Richmond, as one interviewing precinct for the 1970 Senate race, when Harry F. Byrd, Jr., was running as an Independent.

"On our first trip to Broad Rock in 1970, a number of lawns had signs reading, 'Freedom of Choice, Yes; Busing, Never!' and cars bore bumper stickers, 'No Busing, Period!'

"At that time no actual busing had taken place.

"In 1971, black children were bused in to Broad Rock Elementary School and white children were bused out.

"By 1972, the anti-busing lawn placards had been replaced by For Sale signs.

"At one house a teen-ager answered the door and said, 'You can come in, but you'll have to wait till my aunt gets off the phone; she's talking to a real-estate agent about a house they want to buy out in the county.'

"Across the street, an eight-year-old girl came to the door and announced, 'My mother is working now. We're moving away as soon as we sell this house. I don't want to move because all my friends are here, but we have to because of the busing.' "

3. Statistics or Meaning?

[Because of such interviewing and vote analysis, I have repeatedly challenged the concepts advanced by the Survey Research Center of the University of Michigan that recent elections have been decided by those voters who are most easily manipulated.]

"My own election surveys cover the entire period of the Survey Research Center's work. I have noted little evidence to support their conclusion that the indifferent, least involved, least informed voter has exerted a decisive influence in the shifts that have taken place from one election to the next.

"Over the last quarter of a century, my surveys show the voters have been basically rational, in that a sense of self-interest is their strongest single motivation. Ditchdiggers are as rational as college professors and newspaper editors. If they feel their interests under attack, all three groups get quite emotional. Ditchdiggers may be even more rational. I have never interviewed one who thought he was smarter than the president of the United States.

"Always I have found that the main vote shifts between elections have reflected the impacts of what has happened between elections and of the shifting stresses and strains of the great continuing conflicts that agitate the times.

"In recent years a number of political scientists, by using the Survey Research Center's own interviewing data, have begun to challenge earlier interpretations that the voters are irrational."

[Still, the fact that the SRC could make these assertions and that they went unchallenged by political scientists for so long argues strongly, I believe, for the need of competing methodologies and for testing SRC interpretations against the changes in the voting results. Scientific verification should come back to the vote itself.

Perhaps, though, I should go further and point to what I sense may be the "original sin" that differentiates my own work from that of not only the SRC but many other political and social scientists. They seem driven by a compulsion to reduce everything to statistics, as if putting something into figures makes it "scientific," even when the statistics are no better than a poor headline or the theories advanced bear little relation to the voting psychology of real people.

Perhaps the originating division is one's starting point,

whether one is in search of a means of manipulating the voters or a means of understanding the people.

There follows one further extract from my talk before the Historians.]

"For my own part, a myth has grown up over the years, attributing my success in predicting elections to remarkable interviewing skills or superhuman powers of intuition.

"Actually, it has been my system of precinct sampling—not intuition or interviewing skill—that has made it possible for me to cover so much of the country, in successive elections, often alone, or with a few aides.

"The problem that I took on with my pre-election surveys differed from that of orthodox pollsters.

"Predicting elections was never my main objective. My goal—I hope this doesn't sound presumptuous—was to report history and still meet the competition of newspaper deadlines. In setting out to explain the change in voter feeling from one election to the next, I wanted this explanation to hold up years afterwards when historians reread my articles. I also wanted to reach people generally and give the voters a chance to speak out on how they felt. The newspaper feature was headed "The Voters Speak."

"Still, I knew that editors and readers expected me to forecast who would win. To maintain credibility, I had to be right.

"All of these requirements had to be met through a limited number of interviews.

"The system of precinct selection was the key to what success I had. Determining the flow of voting in any precinct usually did not require too many interviews since my mind was programmed with the voting history of every precinct sampled. Repeating the process in scores of precincts, carefully selected to mirror the structure of the electorate, yielded the information needed to determine who would win, and whether by a landslide or a cliff-hanger. That was how I was satisfied to report the outcome—who would win, close or big.

"To have tried to project my findings into percentages would have taken time and energy that could be better devoted to probing more deeply for the meaning of the election.

"This decision to concentrate on meaning rather than statistics may put into better perspective what I have been trying to say about methodology.

"Probably I tend to underestimate, to depreciate what can be done with statistics, because I never extended myself in that direction.

"In turn, I suspect that the quantitative approach in its statistical design cuts itself off from that wonderful world of political sensitivity that can be explored if you are flying in a time-place machine.

"In any case, may I emphasize that nothing now being done through the quantitative approach is incompatible with the use of election returns as a basis of sampling.

"The potential for precise vote calculations is always present in a system of precinct selection, as I demonstrated on a number of election nights and as others have.

"As part of work on my methodology under a Ford Foundation grant, I have done some analysis of the SRC work. I question the importance that the SRC attaches to voter turnout, to the 'information' voters are supposed to need to be 'informed'; also, to what is meant by political involvement and the processes by which election shifts occur.

"The decisive shifts from one election to the next have not come from the indifferent or unconcerned voters. Generally, the level of voter involvement has reflected the level of discontent and concern in the whole nation.

"Some of these differences may be reconciled, leading

perhaps to wider perspectives than either of us have had. The excellent SRC work on the concept of a 'normal party' vote stimulated me to new thoughts, and I can see how this concept can be harmonized with the dynamics of coalition politics."

[This conflict between statistics and meaning, which extends into all polling, seems likely to sharpen rather than ease.

The major public polls—of Gallup and Harris—have been concentrating on improving the percentage accuracy of their final predictions, with significant success.

Also the National Council on Public Polls has been circulating "guidelines" for editors to use in judging political polls. One aim is to discredit polls leaked by partisans. These "guidelines," though, do not insure adequate or even accurate meaning in the established polls.

Many "issues," as with those dealing with Vietnam, cannot be covered in a single question, which is common polling practice. Often as well people interviewed are asked to agree or disagree with prefabricated statements, none of which may express the feelings of the public.

Statistical polls will not yield the understanding we should have of political, social, and economic change. The need will remain for a competing methodology, based on the voting returns, which works out the meaning of change through flexible and intensive interviews of individuals.

Much of what was written in this book was not reported in any standard poll.]

Index